ALLEN'S

AUTHENTICATION

OF

ANCIENT CHINESE

BRONZES

By Anthony J. Allen

Also By The Same Author:
"Allen's Introduction to Later Chinese Porcelain"
"Allen on Fraud"
"Allen's Authentication of Later Chinese Porcelain"

DEDICATION
To my dear wife, Elizabeth.

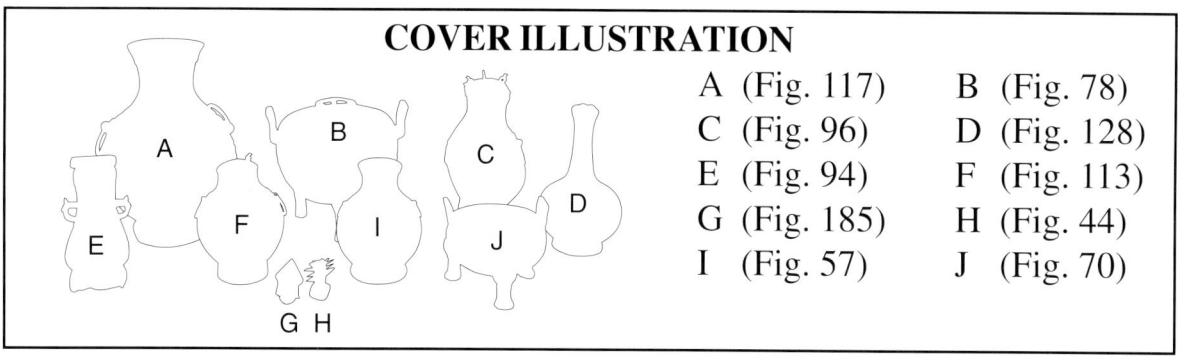

COVER ILLUSTRATION

A (Fig. 117)	B (Fig. 78)
C (Fig. 96)	D (Fig. 128)
E (Fig. 94)	F (Fig. 113)
G (Fig. 185)	H (Fig. 44)
I (Fig. 57)	J (Fig. 70)

Title: "Allen's Authentication of Ancient Chinese Bronzes"

Author: Anthony John Allen

First Edition: November 2001

Photography &
Digital Scanning: B.T. Scanning Ltd

Publisher: Allen's Enterprises Ltd,
P.O. Box 33-194,
Takapuna,
Auckland,
New Zealand

Ph/Fax: +64-9-479-3960
E-mail: Allen.Ent@xtra.co.nz
Web-site: www.allensantiques.com

ISBN No: 0-473-08045-1

COPYRIGHT
All rights reserved. No part of this publication may be reproduced, stored in a retrieval system, or transmitted, in any form or by any means, electronic, mechanical, photocopying, scanning or otherwise, without the prior written permission of the publishers. Such permission, if granted, is subject to a fee, depending on the nature of the use.

Printed In New Zealand

CONTENTS

		Page
PREFACE		4
INTRODUCTION		5
CHAPTER 1	A Cautionary Digression	7
CHAPTER 2	A Brief History of Chinese Bronzes	11
CHAPTER 3	The Chinese Bronze Casting Technique	15
CHAPTER 4	An Outline of Authentication Techniques	19
CHAPTER 5	Indications of Dating from the Shape and Design	21
CHAPTER 6	Metallurgical Analysis	35
CHAPTER 7	X-ray Analysis	39
CHAPTER 8	Thermoluminescence & Carbon 14 Dating	43
CHAPTER 9	High Power Microscopy & Digital Scanning	49
CHAPTER 10	Patination & Corrosion	51
CHAPTER 11	Positive Visual Considerations in Authentication	57
CHAPTER 12	Inscriptions & Inlaid Designs	69
CHAPTER 13	A Catalogue of Affordable Bronzes	73
CHAPTER 14	Fakes & Forgeries & Their Detection	145
CHAPTER 15	Conclusion	157
SELECTED BIBLIOGRAPHY		166
INDEX		169

TABLES INCLUDED WITHIN THE TEXT

TABLE 1	Chinese Dynastic Periods Before AD220	11
TABLE 2	Ancient Bronze Alloy Formulae from the K'ao Kung Chi	15
TABLE 3	Metallurgical Analysis of Ten Samples	36
TABLE 4	Thermoluminescence Dating of Five Samples	46

PREFACE

It is five years now since I wrote my first magazine article on the detection of fake Chinese bronzes, and since that time there has been an extraordinary increase in the number and variety of both fake and genuine ancient Chinese bronzes available. With the possible exception of the Oriental Ceramic Society of Hong Kong's exhibition of 1990, almost nothing in the way of meaningful books or articles in English, that assist in authentication and fake detection, has been written in the past thirty years; since the now out of print ground-breaking published research of the Freer collection, by Pope, Gettens, Cahill & Barnard.

My background is in forensic accounting, notably fraud investigations, and since my retirement I have written two books on later Chinese porcelain. However, my business today, as New Zealand's largest Asian art dealer, is primarily in smuggled Chinese ceramics and bronzes, which I buy legally in Hong Kong. I have no formal training or academic qualifications in metallurgical or chemical analysis, and what information I have learned and impart in this book, is from my own experience.

My dealing activities on the Internet have caused me to run foul of a number of academics, historians, palaeontologists and archaeologists, all of whom believe that the artefacts which I deal in, from dinosaur eggs to bronze vessels, should remain in the ground untouched until a future generation can study them. Archaeological magazines refuse to publish articles on any antique bronze piece that has not got a provenance or pedigree prior to 1973, in a misguided attempt to suppress information that may escalate the trade in smuggled artefacts. Corruption, dishonesty and in some cases just plain incompetence, pervade not only the Chinese antiques trade, but also, regrettably, some areas of the academic and scientific fraternities. Misinformation and disinformation abound.

So this book is written, not from an academic standpoint, but in the interests of all collectors and dealers who wish to acquire these presently available genuine ancient Chinese bronze artefacts. There are no lengthy "auction catalogue-like" descriptions of the pieces illustrated. Nor are the pieces necessarily of museum quality, but more often than not, they are affordable bronzes which are relatively freely available; and thus seldom illustrated in museum publications.

My fervent wish is that I may encourage more collectors and dealers to take advantage of the exciting opportunities that currently exist to collect and preserve for a future generation of collectors, these wonderful ancient Chinese bronze masterpieces; which would otherwise, if academia had its way, rot to nothing in the ground.

INTRODUCTION

My motivation in writing this book is probably most unusual. In early 1999, having closed my antique shop in Auckland, New Zealand, I was faced with the problem of disposing of a shop full of stock, which primarily consisted of antique Chinese porcelain. I started selling on the internet auctions through eBay in America (under the seller name anthonyjallen), and in a very short space of time, such was the initial success of this business, that I was requiring additional stock.

The antique shops of Hong Kong at that time were stocked with masses of burial pottery and bronze artefacts, dating from Neolithic times through to the Ming dynasty, most of them allegedly uncovered through either the flooding in China, the worst in 20 years, or because of the enormous amount of land development being undertaken. The Three Gorges Dam development and raising of the water levels are reported to have revealed numerous burial sites. Coupled with these factors, some of the Chinese peasant population gained access to metal detectors, and Hong Kong was a ready market for their finds; its annexation to China in 1997 resulting in a relaxation of border controls for smuggled antiques.

So I decided that if the Chinese Government authorities in Hong Kong would permit the legal sale and export of smuggled antiques from China, then I would start selling more of these newly available bronze items. I bought a number of bronze swords, followed by other bronze weapons and vessels. Later that year, one of my by now regular bronze-buying U.S. customers started sending his purchases for authentication by a U.S. metallurgical laboratory which claimed competence in authenticating ancient Chinese bronzes. Several bronze swords, to my embarrassment, were declared to be fake, and I was obliged to make a number of refunds.

While I accept that one particular group of swords were modern forgeries, at an early date I began to have misgivings about this laboratory's ability and experience to undertake the evaluations to which they professed competence. The vessels were not referred to by their correct names, and stylistically the dating, which they claimed came from corrosion samples in a data-base, was demonstrably wrong. Several vessels were declared to be fake because of modern tool signature visible under high power magnification, and two of those (Fig. C & E) are illustrated in this book. Others were declared problematic (Fig. D on the cover), in my opinion, because the laboratory proprietor did not have the experience to state otherwise.

This U.S. laboratory cost me thousands of dollars, not just in unnecessary refunds to my customers, but in subsequent freight and travel costs returning items for refund to my suppliers. To add insult to injury, he also ripped me off to the tune of some $US1400 in false and unsubstantiated freight charges and underpaid purchase price on a genuine inlaid sword, which the proprietor simply stole.

By the time that I had refunded the sale price of the allegedly fake swords, I thought that I had escaped the clutches of this charlatan, only to find that he had declared to my customer that one of the two bronze vessels (C on the cover) to be fake, the other (D) problematic, and I reluctantly gave a further refund of $US2,474, subject to them being re-invoiced if I could prove otherwise. I had decided that if these bronzes were fake, then I would stop dealing in them altogether. But how to get them authenticated?

The first step was to take them to Hong Kong, where they were certificated as genuine by the Hong Kong Art Craft Merchants Association. Back in New Zealand, I took both pieces to Clive Jennings, forensic metallurgist and managing director of Metal Test Ltd, who arranged for electron scanning microscopy of the base metal and x-ray analysis. Core samples from a bronze hu vase (F) from the same source, but not tested in America, were thermoluminescence tested by David Price at Wollongong University in Australia. High resolution digital scanning and photography by Neil Beattie of BT Scanning Ltd, all confirmed features supporting an early dating, all in conflict with the opinion of the U.S. laboratory. I record my appreciation to each of these obliging gentlemen, without whose help, this book would not have been possible. Several thousands of dollars out of pocket from this unfortunate experience, but reassured as to the authenticity of the items which I sell, I decided to pass on the information that I had learned, and this book is the end result.

The ten items listed on the cover have been subjected to detailed examination, and many of the pointers for authentication referred to in this book are frequently cross-referenced to one or other of these pieces, by letters A through J, as may be seen on the page 2.

I must also record my appreciation to the following people who assisted in the preparation of this book:
To my very good Hong Kong friend and agent, Leung Hop Tai, without whose assistance, knowledge of antiques, and translation skills, this book would have been impossible.
To John Piscopo in La Grange, Illinois for his support and encouragement.
To Ian McIntyre for the photography.
To Brian Gill who reset the photographs digitally into the text.
To my good friend Geoff Perkins, who voluntarily did the proof reading.
And finally, my wife Elizabeth, whose remarkable tolerance of my collecting passion, has now lasted over 30 years.

CHAPTER 1

A CAUTIONARY DIGRESSION

In my first book, "Allen's Introduction to Later Chinese Porcelain", I started with a similarly titled chapter, the reason being to acquaint novice readers with "peculiarities" of the Chinese antiques scene. Despite the fact that some of these opinions are "politically incorrect", the response from my readers has been overwhelmingly positive.

1.1 The Chinese Language
Unfortunately I do not read Chinese, although I can recognise most Ming and Qing dynastic reign marks, and so for the translation of Chinese characters I am dependent on the translation skills of others. However, the following brief introduction to the Chinese language may be of assistance.

Today, the written language of China is Chinese, the official spoken dialect being the guttural sounding Mandarin (or Putonghua), which is native to the northern Chinese. Mandarin is also the official dialect of Taiwan and Singapore, while in Hong Kong, the "singsong" Cantonese is used. There are also numerous other dialects in the provinces.

The standard modern Chinese script, known as kaishu, is common to most dialects, so that while one Chinese person may not understand the spoken word of another, the written language usually provides a means of communication. Until recently, Chinese was written vertically from right to left, so to understand the Chinese written word, one started with the extreme right hand column, reading vertically downwards, before moving to the top of the next column to the left. Today, especially in newspapers, writing Chinese characters in horizontal lines, as distinct from vertical, and reading from left to right is becoming more common, but again, this is not the universal practice.

Thirty years after the Communist government took control of China in 1949, the system of Romanisation, or transliteration, of Chinese into English, was officially standardised to that known as Pinyin. Chinese words may comprise one or more characters which, under the previously commonly accepted Wade-Giles system of Romanisation, was both phonetically based and spelled. However, the Pinyin system has proved to be a "nightmare"; a ridiculous academic solution to a relatively minor problem. Peking under Pinyin has become Beijing, Taipei is Taibei, Ch'ing has become Qing, and Canton has become Guangzhou. Thus we now have Peking duck and glass, Taipei on aircraft schedules and destinations, but Taibei on many maps, Qing and Ch'ing ceramics, and Canton famille rose. Ting has become ding,

Chou has become Zhou, etc, and to add to the confusion, Chinese scholars, especially in Taiwan, prefer to use the old Wade-Giles system. This is not surprising, given their already difficult problem they face in translating Chinese into English. The Pinyin system adds to these difficulties by arbitrarily stating that some English letters are not pronounced in the traditional English manner. Thus:

        c is pronounced **ts**
        q is pronounced **ch'**
        x is pronounced **s**
        zh is pronounced **j**

Any reader interested in converting between the two systems, will find a useful Pinyin to Wade-Giles table appearing in **Jonathon D. Spence's, "The Search For Modern China"**.

Because the majority of books printed before 1950 used the Wade-Giles (or an alternative system), students of Chinese bronzes now need to learn both systems, and the end result is what happens with idiotic bureaucratic interference; as the translation errors of most Chinese published texts so graphically illustrate. I have reluctantly used the Pinyin system in this book, but where helpful, I have shown the Wade-Giles equivalent in parentheses.

To add further to the confusion, the inscriptions on the ancient Chinese bronzes were frequently written in an ancient hieroglyphic script, often resembling pictographs, the translation of which can be very difficult.

1.2 Chinese Historical Texts

Readers should be alert to the fact that the Chinese historical texts are notoriously unreliable, yet writer after writer refers to them ad nauseum, thus implying that they are accurate descriptions of what actually occurred. Some of these writings may well have been accurate, but their veracity is compromised by the sheer number of patently inaccurate descriptions recorded in most works, even to the present day. As an example, I will in Chapter 3, set out the ancient bronze formula, which modern scientific analysis methods have long since disproved. Yet even as late as 1995, in an otherwise excellent Chinese introductory book, **Li Xueqin in "Chinese Bronzes. A General Introduction"**, seemingly perpetuates the myth that Chinese bronze consisted solely of copper and tin.

1.3 Disinformation

In my experience, I suspect that there can be few fields of study anywhere that have so many divergent opinions as there are to be found with ancient Chinese bronzes. Misinformation and disinformation abound, and the anonymity of the Internet and Internet chat groups, has permitted a number of self-declared experts to spread their nonsense to a wide audience. I am frequently sent e-mail stating such and such a piece I am selling is fake, and in the past two years alone, I have received the following advice:

> *Zinc isn't found in Chinese bronzes before 1700 AD.*
> *All ancient Chinese bronzes have green patina.*
> *If the bronze is brown it must be from the Ming dynasty.*
> *Turquoise inlay does not survive in the ground.*
> *If the lacquer scabbard is still with the Han dynasty sword, it must be fake.*

All of these statements may be either true or false in relation to a specific bronze article, but not as generalisations.

The final determination as to the age or authenticity of a Chinese bronze, in the absence of corroborative scientific evidence, is still likely to be a matter of opinion. Even the experts get it wrong, and to illustrate this point, readers may like to compare the fascinating comments by successive curators of the Freer Gallery, as detailed in **"The Freer Chinese Bronzes", by Pope, Gettens, Cahill & Barnard.**

1.4 Dishonesty

Regrettably, the field of ancient Chinese bronzes is an area for extreme caution, largely as a result of the inherent dishonesty of the native Chinese bronze casters and dealers. I issued the following warning in my first book on later Chinese porcelain, and it is equally, if not more relevant, to ancient Chinese bronzes*: "Novice collectors should be alert to the Chinese practice of cheating. It is not a new practice, but extends back thousands of years, and at the risk of attracting the asinine attention of the Race Relations Office, I suspect that it is as accepted with them as perhaps rice and vegetables is with dinner".*

In Hollywood Road and Cat Street in Hong Kong, the main antique area in the city, over 90% of the dealers stock fakes, in many cases intermingled with their genuine antique pieces. Most will try and sell the fake as a genuine antique. In Taiwan, Singapore, Macau and China the percentage is closer to 100%. Fortunately there are some honest Chinese dealers, like my friend Mr. Tai, or the half dozen other Hong Kong dealers who are my regular suppliers. The trick is to find such people.

Dishonesty is not restricted just to the Chinese dealers. There are a number of patently dishonest Western dealers as well, some of whom operate on the Internet, even claiming to have thermoluminescence test reports to support their assertions. To add to the problems of dishonesty, there are the charlatan authentication bureaus and testing laboratories, the activities of one of which I mentioned earlier. And the dishonest dealer or collector who with photocopier or scanner, doctors or reproduces genuine laboratory reports so as to appear that they relate to a fake which they are selling. If one expects dishonesty, then one will not be surprised when it is confronted. "Forewarned is forearmed".

1.5 The Error Ratio

If any reader is going to get into the field of ancient Chinese bronze collecting, and I sincerely hope that nothing that I have said will discourage anybody, then the first thing to be accepted is that there will be mistakes. I openly tell my customers that I try to work on a 1% or less error rate, and this would in fact be closer to zero, but for the fact that I speculate. As I do not want people approaching me in years to come with something for refund, which I have mistakenly sold as genuine, I usually sell with a 180 day return warranty. After 180 days, if the buyer has not proved that it is other than as listed, the warranty expires and it is then the buyer's problem. However, for a small additional charge I will issue non-transferable lifetime certificates of authenticity.

Today, my errors are largely confined to not spotting restoration, my suppliers narrowed down to a select few whose honesty I can trust. Despite the fact that we sell over 2,000 Chinese antiques per annum, it is over 18 months since a fake of any description was returned to me.

Most Chinese dealers do not even offer that guarantee. Of course, if I am 100% certain, and have thermoluminescence test reports etc to support it, I offer an unqualified guarantee. If you want to be certain of your purchase, then my advice is to buy from respected dealers who at least give you this opportunity for refund. But if you want to occasionally make some extraordinarily good purchase, then you will need to take the risk that I do, and periodically speculate; for the best buys may turn up in a provincial auction or antique shop, where the proprietor has no experience of them.

1.6 A Considered Opinion

I will in this book attempt to show a number of features that will indicate that a bronze may be genuine. I stress the word **may**, because almost all of the features which I will discuss can be duplicated by clever copyists. And the most difficult bronze to authenticate is likely to be the one that has been cleaned of its patina, or perhaps been buried in an atmosphere where corrosion did not occur. It is not necessarily just one pointer that gives a positive or negative confirmation of authenticity, but a number of them.

Readers must remember, that almost every feature of a genuine ancient bronze can be duplicated by today's bronze casters. However, the cost of replication, especially of genuine patination, will usually be too high to be justified. So the trick is to not only observe the features one would expect to see on an ancient bronze, but to look for those features which one would expect to see, but which are not there; and then observe features which one would not expect to see. And finally, remember also, the fateful statement, *"For almost every rule there will be an exception"*.

CHAPTER 2

A BRIEF HISTORY OF CHINESE BRONZES

(Shang To Han Dynasty; 1766 BC to 220 AD)

Even today, historians cannot agree as to when bronze casting first started in China. This is not surprising, given the fact they also do not even know for certain when the Shang dynasty started or finished, the majority consensus until very recently, accepting a circa 16th century BC starting point, and a circa 1050 BC finish. Several Chinese authors have now narrowed the starting and finishing dates of these early dynasties to specific years, and with some hesitation I have adopted these dates in this book. But what is certain, is that during the Shang dynasty the Chinese bronze workers had become sufficiently skilled to be able to make most elaborate bronze castings, in some cases so elaborate that even with today's high technology, they are difficult to reproduce.

Bronze vessels are usually dated to the dynasty, or period of the dynasty, in which they were made, so as a first step, the novice collector of ancient Chinese bronzes should familiarise themselves with these.

Table 1	Table Of Chinese Dynastic Periods Before AD220.			
	Xia Dynasty:	2205	to	1766 BC
	Shang Dynasty:	1766	to	1122 BC
	Zhou Dynasty:			
	Western Zhou	1122	to	771 BC
	Eastern Zhou	770	to	256 BC
	Spring & Autumn	770	to	476 BC
	Warring States	475	to	221 BC
	Qin Dynasty:	221	to	206 BC
	Han Dynasty:			
	Western Han	206 BC	to	9 AD
	Wang Mang Interregnum	9 AD	to	25 AD
	Eastern Han	25 AD	to	220 AD

Readers will find in some books, reference to the period of the Erlitou culture, which if the ancient texts are to believed, existed as part of the preceding Xia dynasty in the period circa 19th to the 16th century BC. There has, until recently, been much debate as to whether in fact the Xia was a legendary dynasty, but recent scientific excavations are tending to support the claims that the Xia did exist.

The succeeding Shang dynasty is sometimes split into the following periods:

    Period of Erligang culture (Zhengzhou phase)   16th to 14th century BC
    Period of Yinxu culture (Anyang phase)   13th to 11th century BC

The Anyang phase reputedly lasted for 273 years, and archaeological study of the Yin ruins, near Anyang has been ongoing intermittently since the late 1920s.

Metal casting undoubtedly started long before the Shang dynasty, probably beginning with copper or lead smelting, perhaps as early as 3,000BC. Then by experimentation, gradually introducing tin to the copper, once the advantages of tin became known, they made bronze, for tin not only lowers the melting point, but also hardens the alloy. Whoever discovered the bronze alloy first and applied it to weapons casting must have enjoyed a considerable advantage, because their spears and axe heads now held an edge. The addition of the lead component, also reduced the melting point, enabling designs of greater detail to be cast, and no doubt significantly reduced the cost. It would be almost 5,000 years before the dangers of lead poisoning would be appreciated.

The Chinese people, since Neolithic times, had believed in an afterlife, and the dead were often buried with the articles and luxuries which they had enjoyed in life. These possessions included not only bronze vessels and weapons, but also pottery and jade articles. Also, cowrie shells (money), jewellery, and personal accoutrements of bone, stone and ivory. By the Han dynasty (starting 206 BC) articles of lacquer, fabric, iron and wood had made their appearance.

For much of the Shang and Zhou dynasties, the wealthy aristocracy also included sacrifices in the burials, and it is not uncommon to find the deceased's favourite concubine, his slaves, and even horses and dogs. This accounts for the finding of other bronze items; horse bells, bridle bits and dog collars etc in close proximity to bronze burial vessels. The wasteful burial practices of this early period were eventually outlawed, the live slaves and the servants and animals being replaced in the Han dynasty by pottery replicas.

The Xia dynasty, which preceded the Shang, was overthrown by the latter in circa 1,766 BC. China was a slave society at this time, and would remain so until the end of the Western Zhou, when private land ownership would be introduced. The head of each tribe is usually referred to as a king, for the first proclaimed Emperor would not appear until the Qin dynasty in 221BC. Both the Shang and the Zhou dynasties were periods of great civil unrest, and the tribes' boundaries extended and retracted as wars were won or lost, in several instances forcing the removal of the capital to another city.

In the Shang dynasty, a practice of ancestor worship using relatively standardised bronze vessel forms seems to have evolved. The rituals required vessels of particular form, and there were a series of strict rules adhered to as regards the type and number of pieces allocated to the ruling hierarchy. For example, by the Western Zhou period (1122 to 771 BC), the bronze tripod ding was one of the most important ritual vessels. Quoting from the catalogue which accompanied the 1999 Warring States Treasures exhibition, *"A set of tripods of graduated sizes was called sheng ding, or lao ding. According to ancient texts on rituals, protocol in the Western Zhou period stipulated that the king was entitled to nine ding, a feudal vassal seven ding, a senior officer five ding, a common officer three or one ding."*

Bronze at this period was a very valuable metal, and the importance of a Chinese family was reflected in the size and grandeur of their bronze vessels. While the Shang bronzes seem mainly to have been used for ritual purposes, and frequently buried with the dead, by the Eastern Zhou, numbers of (in some cases substantial) bronze vessels were being made for daily use. Others were made, not for burial, but for paying their respects to the ancestors.

Those who could not afford bronze, occasionally used lead substitutes. Others used cheaply cast bronzes, like the fanghu vase (E on the cover). As the centuries progressed, bronze seems to have become more freely available, and it was used for a greater variety of uses; garment hooks, mirrors, lamps, horse and chariot fittings, etc. With the introduction of iron in the Eastern Zhou dynasty, a lot of traditional bronze uses became redundant. Swords were made with iron blades, although the guards and handles (grips and pommels) were usually still of bronze.

The bronzes that are available to us today have come in the main from two sources; either the tombs and graves of the dead, or the troves of bronze that were sometimes buried at times of great civil unrest. Such must have been the haste that these bronze owners departed, that they frequently seem to have just carelessly thrown the artefacts into a pit, undoubtedly intending to collect their treasure at some more peaceful time. This suggests that it was the bronze metal itself, rather than the artefact (or its sentimental value), that was the valuable commodity. From my observations, probably 90% or more of these bronzes have sustained some damage, necessitating restoration, caused either from the effects of long burial, or intentional damage before burial.

The wealth of genuine ancient Chinese bronze items currently available, has resulted in a substantial drop in market prices, and this drop has probably been exacerbated by the activities of the modern day copyist, who has greatly unsettled the market. The Chinese have been faking or embellishing these early bronzes for at least two thousand years, and in the centuries ahead, I have no doubt that collectors will be seeking some of the modern day masterpieces. But for the present, these fakes are a problem for all who collect or deal in them.

Many of these earlier fakes entered our museum collections at an early date last century, where they remain in some cases still unrecognised. The focus of this book is not on these early fakes, but rather on the ones being made in present day China, and often sold side by side with the genuine excavated artefact.

For those readers wanting to explore the history of ancient Chinese bronze casting further than I have given in this briefest of summaries, there is a wealth of books on the subject.

CHAPTER 3
THE CHINESE BRONZE CASTING TECHNIQUE

In my experience there is widespread confusion, and in some cases disagreement, as to the methods used by the early bronze metal workers to fabricate their bronzes. Fortunately, this confusion has caused problems for the modern copyists, for many of their reproductions may be identified immediately by the use of a non-traditional method.

The Western standard for bronze was usually 90% copper and 10% tin. As early as 1904, Stephen Bushell was quoting the proportions of copper and tin employed in the fabrication of bronze objects during the Zhou (Chou) dynasty, as handed down in the K'ao kung chi, a contemporary work on the industries of the period.

Table 2 Ancient Bronze Alloy Formulae From The K'ao Kung Chi		
Item:	**Copper%**	**Tin%**
Bells, cauldrons, gongs, sacrificial vessels & utensils	83.33	16.67
Axes & Hatchets	80.00	20.00
Halberd heads & trident spears	75.00	25.00
Swords & agricultural equipment	66.67	33.33
Arrow heads & curved knives etc	60.00	40.00
Mirrors	50.00	50.00

While in Bushell's case he may have not had the scientific equipment to enable the alloy to be tested, there can be no further justification for continuing this myth. Many academics, persist in quoting these hopelessly unreliable Chinese historical records, for all aspects of bronze and ceramic history, and in the case of the alleged alloy mix, they are demonstrably incorrect.

The actual bronze formula, as I will demonstrate in a later chapter, consisted of hugely varying percentages of copper, tin and (usually) lead, occasionally with probably unintentional traces of other elements, notably silver, iron or zinc.

Unlike their Western counterparts, except perhaps in the Neolithic period, bronze was not worked by smithying, but by casting in sectional clay moulds. The fine northern clays of China enabled very fine imprints of designs to be taken and transferred to the bronze, which was poured into the gaps between the clay moulds, which were themselves held apart (if the vessel was thin-walled) by small bronze spacers (or chaplets). So there are two recurring features of ancient bronze casting, appearing in the majority of ancient bronze vessels; mould lines and spacers, the latter sometimes only visible by x-ray. I stress the word **majority,** because there are exceptions to this statement.

Fig.1 Mould Lines on an Ancient Ding   **Fig.2 Spacers on an Ancient Hu**

Fig. 1 shows the underside of a Spring and Autumn period lidded ding (B on the cover). Note, not only the mould lines, but also the applied hollow legs, and the traces of fire (carbon), all positive signs for authentication. Fig. 2 shows the clearly visible spacers on a Warring States period hu vase. (I on the cover). Note also the inward bending mouth rim, another positive sign for authentication.

Other features to look for indicating the ancient casting technique, are sprue marks where the metal was poured, and vent marks (in this case on the sides of the foot rim), where gases escaped, the vent marks of which are visible in Fig.3, also from the Warring States hu vase (I on the cover).

Fig.3 Sprue & Vent Marks on an Ancient Hu

I have inspected these marks very carefully, before arriving at the conclusion that they are in fact sprue and vent marks. The double V or (7) mark in the centre, appears to have been cut off, suggesting that it was a sprue or pouring mark, and not just some identifying symbol. The vent marks (arrowed) are regularly spaced, and of triangular shape, rather than the more squarish-shaped spacers to be found in the upper neck of this vase.

In addition to sectional mould casting, the ancient bronze makers used a variety of techniques to overcome the design shortcomings of this method of manufacture, by attaching lugs (handles) and legs etc by sometimes complicated dovetailing or recasting, and even with a system of welding. More detailed finishing was also done after firing by polishing, hand-finishing; or inlay with glass, silver, lacquer, copper, gold or semiprecious stones.

Some of the more ornate bronzes show that the design was undercut, making the width of the bottom of the cut wider than at the surface. This must have meant that the mould had to be broken off the bronze, and in these instances anyway, can seldom have been re-used. Among the pieces that I have had available to photograph, is a bronze ding, the base of which appears to have been made from a re-used mould, (not visible in Fig. 4) because traces of the original leiwen or thunder pattern remain.

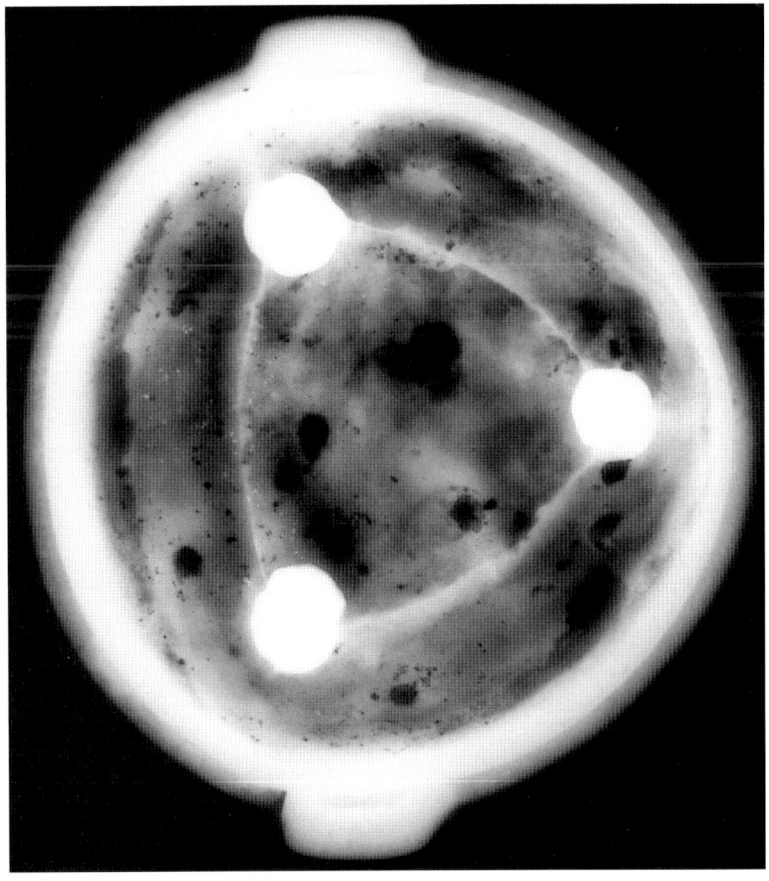

Fig.4 X-ray of Underside of a Western Zhou Ding

Note again, the to be expected mould lines as well.

For the most detailed bronze castings, certainly from the 6th century BC, the cire perdue or lost wax process was occasionally used, the process using as the name suggests, bronze replacement for the by then melted wax mould. But from the Western Han dynasty (206BC to 9AD), on many of the vessels from this period, while spacers are still used, the mould lines disappear, suggesting either a different method of casting, or a higher standard of finishing. The massive hu vase (A on the cover) is such an example. The appearance of cast iron moulds at this time, may have resulted in closer fitting joins, as well as enabling the moulds to be reused. They may also explain the virtual absence of elaborate designs in the Han dynasty, the majority of vessels being plain in comparison with their earlier counterparts.

The method of making the legs and lugs on the later vessels, will often immediately show a piece to be modern, for they were not usually cast in solid bronze. I have to date seen only one modern made bronze with a clay cored leg or lug, and this should be detectable if not by visual examination, then by either x-ray or drilling.

A much more detailed description of the ancient casting techniques may be found in the following book:
Barnard, N: "Bronze Casting & Bronze Alloys In Ancient China"

CHAPTER 4
AN OUTLINE OF AUTHENTICATION TECHNIQUES

I mentioned earlier, but repeat again, the three primary considerations that collectors and dealers should in my opinion assess, to determine the authenticity or otherwise of an ancient Chinese bronze:
1. The appearance of features one would expect to see on an ancient bronze.
2. The absence of features one would expect to see on an ancient bronze.
3. The appearance of features one would not expect to see on an ancient bronze.

I have devoted a short chapter to each of the following topics, which can in some cases assist in this regard.

4.1 Dating Indications From The Shape and Design
This is far too comprehensive a subject to adequately cover within the confines of this book, but in Chapter 5 I will attempt to provide brief outlines of the most common shapes and forms, and the time periods which each shape stylistically fits into. In the past 30 years, such has been the extent of new discoveries in China, there has been a huge increase in the number of ancient shapes and designs known to us. So we cannot always immediately reject as modern, every bronze that does not conform to a set form. However, readers should appreciate that animal form vessels, inlaid figures and vessels, and inscriptions, considerably increase the price or value of the piece. As a consequence, the copyist often fabricates such items, or occasionally embellishes genuine early bronzes with later inlay, inscriptions or designs. Often, in my experience, these pieces will be given away by their low market price. I will expand on this subject in a later chapter.

4.2 Metallurgical and Chemical Analysis
In my opinion, knowing the metallurgical composition of a bronze, by whatever process it is done, is seldom going to confirm the authenticity of the piece in question. With today's modern technology, the alloy content of bronzes of antiquity can be duplicated at will. There is also the possibility that old bronze scraps can be re-smelted, and while I have heard unofficially that this is occurring, having seen the Chinese ability to repair broken bronzes, I doubt very much that this is happening to any large extent.

4.3 X-ray Analysis
This has proven to be the most consistently reliable, as well as the least expensive, of the scientific tests that we applied. X-rays can show a number of ancient bronze casting features, not always visible to the naked eye, including casting flaws, spacers, old (or new) repairs, air bubbles, clay cores etc.

4.4 Thermoluminescence and Carbon 14 Dating

Either of these testing procedures may confirm that the bronze in question is not new, but there is usually to be some doubt that the age determined is actually the age of the casting. For example, the clay core inside a ding's leg may have subsequently stood in a fire; or a tree root may have attached itself say 500 years later.

4.5 High Power Microscopy and Digital Scanning

Owing to my own, admittedly limited, experiences with high power microscopy, I have grave reservations as to its reliability. The main use of high power microscopy is in the detection of machine tool signatures and false patination, but for it to be accepted as a reliable indicator of a fake, the viewer needs to then determine that the machine tools were not used in a repair (or commonly, for cleaning off the corrosion); nor the false patination used to cover a repair or fault, on a genuine ancient piece. On the other hand, I have found high power digital scanning to be quite helpful in observing genuine indicators of age; eg. ancient repairs, or tree roots, wood, fibres, textiles etc, embedded in the corrosion.

4.6 Patination and Corrosion

I have heard several foundries claim that they can replicate any ancient bronze patina, and while this may be true of the colour, the build-up of centuries of natural corrosion, is a much more time-consuming and expensive process. In a later chapter on fakes I will illustrate some very good quality modern patinas. Easier to spot immediately as fake, are the flaking cerussite coloured grey-white patinas, which are used on a lot of the less expensive new bronzes. Much more difficult to duplicate, are the combined cuprite, malachite and azurite patinas found on many genuine pieces.

4.7 A Considered Opinion

Again I must end this chapter on this title, for at the end of the day, a positive or negative attribution is going to be a matter of considered opinion. The most sophisticated scientific testing procedures can be falsified or misinterpreted, and one's evaluation must consider even that possibility. However, by considering the factors which I enumerate it in this book, it should in the majority of cases be able to be established, one way or the other, the authenticity or otherwise of the bronze in question.

CHAPTER 5

INDICATIONS OF DATING FROM THE SHAPE AND DESIGN

Two of the most popular designs of ancient China, still popular to this day, are the taotie (or lion mask), usually to be found in combination with the leiwen (or thunder pattern). There are numerous variants of the leiwen design, ranging from that of Fig. 6, to the more usual leiwen of Fig. 101.

Fig. 5 Taotie Design
(From Lidded Hu F)

Fig. 6 Stylised Leiwen Design
(From Fig. I)

For the novice collector or dealer, the variations in these designs between the Shang and the Han dynasties is difficult to grasp. Readers interested in comparison, may like to view the comments in the two volume **Freer Chinese Bronzes** referred to earlier.

However, in my experience, the shapes of the vessels themselves, in conjunction with their design, can give a much better clue to a possible dating. Obviously, any of these shapes could be (and are) fabricated today, so design alone will not be of much assistance in authenticating the age.

I have listed these vessels by Chinese name, in alphabetical order, with an approximate indication of age. Please be aware however, that as new discoveries are made, these approximate datings may require revision. There are also numerous other vessels, and variants of these vessels, which I have not shown.

5.1 Ding

The ding was a food vessel used for cooking, and genuine examples often show signs of burning on the undersides. The standard ding had three legs, while the four-legged variety was known as fang ding, and a three-legged variation, with goat teat-like underside (and round legs), was known as li ding. Many examples had two lug handles, and later (especially late Zhou) dings sometimes had lids.

```
1600BC      1400BC      1200BC      1000BC      800BC      600BC      400BC      200BC      0      200AD
................Shang.............../.................W. Zhou.............../...Spring &.../...Warring/Qin/W. Han......../..........E.Han...
                                                                        Autumn         States
```

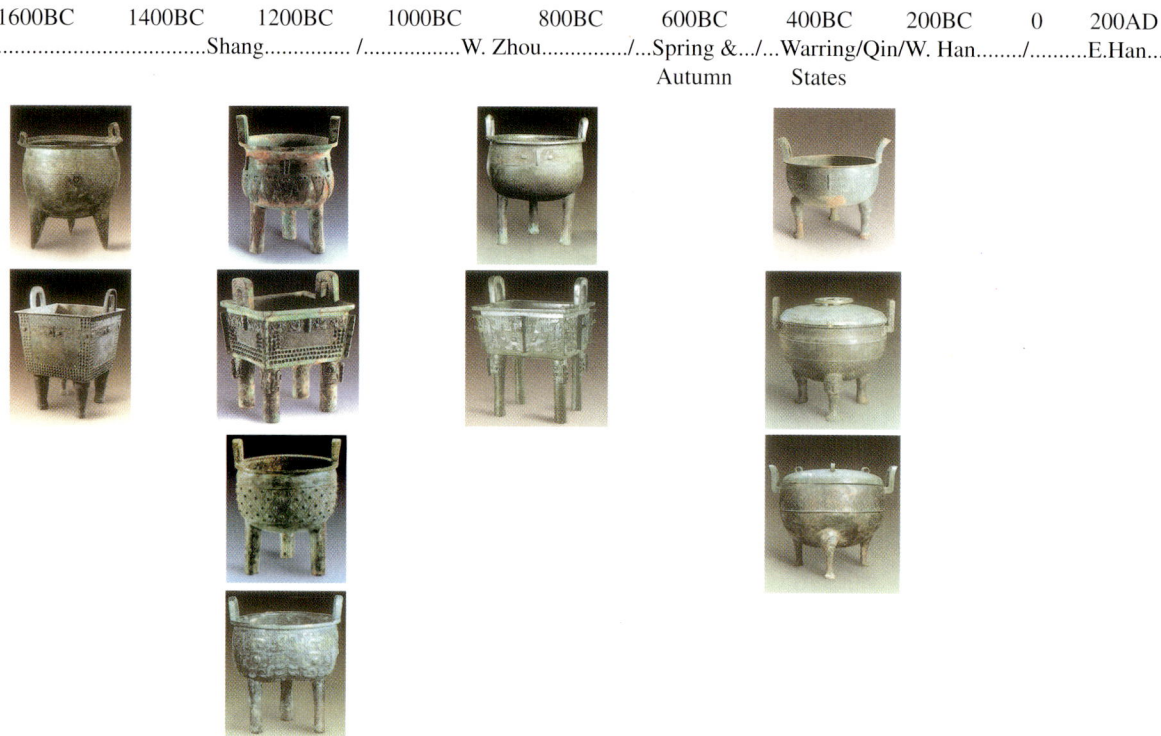

5.2 Dou

The dou was a pedestal based and lidded food vessel, found from the late Zhou dynasty.

```
1600BC      1400BC      1200BC      1000BC      800BC      600BC      400BC      200BC      0      200AD
................Shang.............../.................W. Zhou.............../...Spring &.../...Warring/Qin/W. Han......../..........E.Han...
                                                                        Autumn         States
```

5.3 Dui

The dui (tui) is the old Chinese name for a globe-shaped cooking vessel, similar to a ding, and used for cooking food. It dates from the Spring and Autumn period.

```
1600BC     1400BC     1200BC     1000BC     800BC      600BC      400BC     200BC      0        200AD
..................................Shang............../.................W. Zhou.............../...Spring &.../...Warring/Qin/W. Han......./..........E.Han...
                                                                         Autumn        States
```

5.4 Fang Lei

The fang lei is a rare and valuable lidded ceremonial wine vessel, of rounded tapering quadrilateral form, dating to the late Shang and probably early Zhou.

```
1600BC     1400BC     1200BC     1000BC     800BC      600BC      400BC     200BC      0        200AD
..................................Shang............../.................W. Zhou.............../...Spring &.../...Warring/Qin/W. Han......./..........E.Han...
                                                                         Autumn        States
```

5.5 Fang Yi

The fang yi is also a rare and valuable ceremonial wine vessel, of house form, and dates to the late Shang and early Zhou. Because of its high value, it is frequently copied today.

1600BC   1400BC   1200BC   1000BC   800BC   600BC   400BC   200BC   0   200AD
................................Shang.............. /................W. Zhou.............../...Spring &.../...Warring/Qin/W. Han......../..........E.Han...
                                                                        Autumn   States

5.6 Fu

The fu was a rectangular box-shaped food vessel, with angular sloping sides, usually on a four legged base. It is found in both the early and late Zhou periods. The name is also given to a cauldron.

1600BC   1400BC   1200BC   1000BC   800BC   600BC   400BC   200BC   0   200AD
................................Shang.............. /................W. Zhou.............../...Spring &.../...Warring/Qin/W. Han......../..........E.Han...
                                                                        Autumn   States

5.7 Gong

The gong, sometimes referred to as the "tiger guang", was a lidded ceremonial wine jug. The lid was frequently decorated with a tiger's head. It is one of the most expensive, and most frequently copied, of all of the Shang dynasty bronzes.

```
1600BC      1400BC      1200BC      1000BC      800BC      600BC      400BC      200BC      0      200AD
................................Shang.............. /................W. Zhou............../...Spring &.../...Warring/Qin/W. Han......./..........E.Han...
                                                                     Autumn          States
```

5.8 Gu

The gu was a tall trumpet-mouthed wine cup, dating to the Shang and early Zhou periods. A recurring feature of many (but not all) of these cups, is a cross-shaped hole on either side of the lower section, just below the narrowest point. It is thought that these were for some sort of brackets to hold the mould in place during the pour.

```
1600BC      1400BC      1200BC      1000BC      800BC      600BC      400BC      200BC      0      200AD
.....................Shang.............. /................W. Zhou............../...Spring &.../...Warring/Qin/W. Han......./..........E.Han...
                                                                     Autumn          States
```

 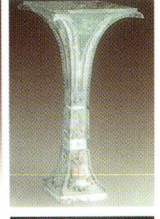

5.9 Gui

The gui was a large (usually) handled food bowl, often lidded, and dates from Shang to late Zhou.

```
1600BC    1400BC    1200BC    1000BC    800BC      600BC     400BC    200BC    0    200AD
.............................Shang.............../.................W. Zhou................/...Spring &.../...Warring/Qin/W. Han........./..........E.Han...
                                                                    Autumn      States
```

5.10 He

The he was a tripod-based and spouted lidded wine jug, which dates from the Shang to the late Zhou periods. However, the same name is also given to a large oval-shaped wine cup or bowl, which usually has two ring handles on an otherwise undecorated body (See Fig.112).

```
1600BC    1400BC    1200BC    1000BC    800BC      600BC     400BC    200BC    0    200AD
.............................Shang.............../.................W. Zhou................/...Spring &.../...Warring/Qin/W. Han........./..........E.Han...
                                                                    Autumn      States
```

5.11 Hu

The hu was a lidded jar (or vase) used to hold wine, and dates from the late Shang to the Han dynasty. Narrowing to the top, it could be round, oval or rectangular. A well known variant is the fang hu, which is a (usually) slightly curving quadrilateral in shape. Another variant is the "garlic headed" hu, which seems to have appeared in the Warring States period.

```
1600BC     1400BC     1200BC     1000BC     800BC     600BC     400BC     200BC     0     200AD
................................Shang.............. /..................W. Zhou................/...Spring &.../...Warring/Qin/W. Han......../..........E.Han...
                                                                          Autumn          States
```

5.12 Jia

The jia was a slender tripod-legged wine cup, dating to the Shang dynasty, and usually adorned with two protruding vertical prongs.

```
1600BC     1400BC     1200BC     1000BC     800BC     600BC     400BC     200BC     0     200AD
................................Shang.............. /..................W. Zhou................/...Spring &.../...Warring/Qin/W. Han......../..........E.Han...
                                                                          Autumn          States
```

5.13 Jian

The jian was a wash basin, somewhat deeper than a pan, usually found with a rim to the edge, and taotie solid cast handles. It dates to the Eastern Zhou dynasties and later.

```
1600BC    1400BC    1200BC    1000BC    800BC    600BC    400BC    200BC    0    200AD
................................Shang.............. /...............W. Zhou............../...Spring &.../...Warring/Qin/W. Han......./..........E.Han...
                                                                   Autumn       States
```

5.14 Jiao

The jiao was a wine vessel, similar to the jue and jia, but in place of a spout had two symmetrical points and a lid. It dates to the Shang and early Zhou dynasties.

```
1600BC    1400BC    1200BC    1000BC    800BC    600BC    400BC    200BC    0    200AD
................................Shang.............. /...............W. Zhou............../...Spring &.../...Warring/Qin/W. Han......./..........E.Han...
                                                                   Autumn       States
```

5.15 Jue

The jue is similar to the jia, but has a pouring lip, similar to that of some modern cream jugs. Used for wine, it dates from the early Shang to the early Zhou period.

1600BC   1400BC   1200BC   1000BC   800BC   600BC   400BC   200BC   0   200AD
.............................Shang.........../............. ....W. Zhou......./.. ...Spring & ...../.....Warring./Qin./W. Han.../....E.Han.../
                                                                  Autumn   States

5.16 Lei

The lei was a bulbous jar, used to store wine, and dates from the early Shang to the Han dynasty.

1600BC   1400BC   1200BC   1000BC   800BC   600BC   400BC   200BC   0   200AD
.................................Shang.............. /.................W. Zhou.............../...Spring &.../...Warring/Qin/W. Han......../..........E.Han...
                                                                  Autumn   States

5.17 Li

The li (or li ding) was a three-legged food vessel, very similar to a ding, but with a lobed undersides, roughly in the form of goat teats. It dates from the Shang to early Zhou dynasties.

```
1600BC     1400BC     1200BC     1000BC     800BC      600BC      400BC      200BC      0          200AD
....................Shang.............. /................W. Zhou............../...Spring &.../...Warring/Qin/W. Han........./..........E.Han...
                                                                    Autumn        States
```

5.18 Pan

The pan is a shallow water basin, found from early Shang to late Zhou, and probably later.

```
1600BC     1400BC     1200BC     1000BC     800BC      600BC      400BC      200BC      0          200AD
....................Shang.............. /................W. Zhou............../...Spring &.../...Warring/Qin/W. Han........./..........E.Han...
                                                                    Autumn        States
```

5.19 Pou

The pou was a rounded food bowl, found from the Shang to the Zhou dynasties, its neck opening being narrower than its width.

1600BC   1400BC   1200BC   1000BC   800BC   600BC   400BC   200BC   0   200AD
................................Shang.............. /.................W. Zhou.............../...Spring &.../...Warring/Qin/W. Han......../..........E.Han...
                                                                    Autumn   States

5.20 Yan (Or Xian)

The yan was a two (or three) section food vessel, comprising a tripod based pot, a fixed or detachable steamer, and in later periods anyway, a lid. It is found in varying shapes from early Shang to Han dynasties.

1600BC   1400BC   1200BC   1000BC   800BC   600BC   400BC   200BC   0   200AD
................................Shang.............. /.................W. Zhou.............../...Spring &.../...Warring/Qin/W. Han......../..........E.Han...
                                                                    Autumn   States

5.21 Yi

The yi was a three or four legged wine jug, similar in some cases to today's gravy boat, and dating to the Western Zhou dynasty and later.

```
1600BC     1400BC     1200BC     1000BC     800BC      600BC      400BC      200BC      0          200AD
................................Shang............../................W. Zhou............../...Spring &.../...Warring/Qin/W. Han......../..........E.Han...
                                                                          Autumn        States
```

5.22 You

The you was a lidded wine jar with an overhanging handle. Found from the early Shang to the late Zhou, they often have elaborate high relief designs. They are one of the more common faked designs.

```
1600BC     1400BC     1200BC     1000BC     800BC      600BC      400BC      200BC      0          200AD
................................Shang............../................W. Zhou............../...Spring &.../...Warring/Qin/W. Han......../..........E.Han...
                                                                          Autumn        States
```

5.23 Yu

The yu was a deepish food bowl, sometimes with handles, dating from late Shang to Han dynasties.

```
1600BC    1400BC    1200BC    1000BC    800BC    600BC    400BC    200BC    0    200AD
................................Shang.............../.................W. Zhou.............../...Spring &.../...Warring/Qin/W. Han........./..........E.Han...
                                                                     Autumn      States
```

5.24 Zhan

The zhan was a lidded food vessel, somewhat similar to a ding, but with a circular handle above, sometimes with circular lugs attaching, indicating that the lid could be tied to the base. Zhan date from the early Eastern Zhou.

```
1600BC    1400BC    1200BC    1000BC    800BC    600BC    400BC    200BC    0    200AD
................................Shang.............../.................W. Zhou.............../...Spring &.../...Warring/Qin/W. Han........./..........E.Han...
                                                                     Autumn      States
```

5.25 Zhi
The zhi was a wine beaker, dating from the Western Zhou.

```
1600BC     1400BC     1200BC     1000BC     800BC     600BC     400BC     200BC     0     200AD
......................Shang.............../.................W. Zhou.............../...Spring &.../...Warring/Qin/W. Han......./..........E.Han...
                                                                        Autumn        States
```

5.25 Zun
The zun was a flaring-mouthed wine jar which in some styles looks more like a Qing dynasty spittoon. It dates from the Shang to the Han dynasties. The same name is used for a bird-shaped wine vessel from the late Zhou dynasty. And to add to the confusion, Rawson & Bunker also use the same name to describe a circular lidded vessel, adorned with taotie handles, three lugs and three feet, which dates from the Spring and Autumn period.

```
1600BC     1400BC     1200BC     1000BC     800BC     600BC     400BC     200BC     0     200AD
......................Shang.............../.................W. Zhou.............../...Spring &.../...Warring/Qin/W. Han......./..........E.Han...
                                                                        Autumn        States
```

34

CHAPTER 6

METALLURGICAL ANALYSIS

Having read the earlier treatises on Chinese bronze metallurgical analyses by Barnard & Pope, I decided that I would undertake my own research, in order to see if I could reach any more meaningful conclusions than what these earlier researchers had achieved. I have absolutely no doubt that my method of testing will be dismissed as amateurish by some sectors of the academic community.

I selected ten different bronzes from my current stock available to me at the time (Fig.7 & Cover), and subjected them to a variety of tests and examinations, details of which I shall expand upon in this and later chapters.

Fig. 7 Ten Ancient Chinese Bronze Artefacts

After consultations with Clive Jennings of Metal Test Ltd, having first removed the surface layers of corrosion, we took a drill sample from some less conspicuous part of each item. The drill samples were then subjected to analysis by scanning electron microscopy (SEM), with an energy dispersive x-ray attachment, by Industrial Research Ltd, the privatised arm of the former New Zealand Government run Department of Scientific and Industrial Research.

Like the majority of readers, I suspect, I was totally out of my depth with this science, so all I could do was await the results of the testing.

#	Description	Approx. Age	Size	Copper %	Tin %	Lead %	Other %
	Table 3 Ten Ancient Bronze Artefacts Selected For Metallurgical Analysis						
A	Massive Hu Vase	2000 - 2200	52H	74.25	8.74	17.01	-
B	Lidded Ding	2400 - 2500	34D	60.03	7.12	32.21	.65
C	Lidded Fanghu Vase	2200 - 2400	42H	72.70	7.23	20.06	-
D	Garlic Head Vase	2200 - 2400	37H	54.21	4.37	41.42	-
E	Lidded Fanghu Vase	2500 - 2700	31H	53.40	8.50	38.10	-
F	Lidded Hu Vase	2300 - 2500	30H	60.83	9.76	27.50	1.91
G	Spear Head	3000 - 3200	25L	42.63	-	56.08	1.29
H	Sword Handle	2100 - 2300	21L	55.94	5.20	38.86	-
I	Hu Vase	2200 - 2400	28H	45.19	5.65	49.16	-
J	Tripod Ding	2800 - 3000	24D	47.73	7.34	43.91	1.02

The results (Table 3) were certainly not what we were expecting, as the lead percentages were considerably higher than had been reported by Barnard & Pope; but who was prepared to argue with an electron scanning microscope? I decided, just to confirm the results, to have two (F & J) of the drill samples double-checked for lead content by the traditional "wet testing" method.

The tripod ding (J) had previously been analysed by the laboratory in New Mexico, U.S.A., by what process I am not certain, but as it was non invasive, it must have been by surface testing only. I then had three allegedly scientific results for the lead content for comparison:

Lead Content	**S.E.M.**	**Wet**	**U.S.A.**
Lidded Hu Vase (F)	27.50%	16.2%	N/A
Tripod Ding (J)	43.91%	17.8%	Trace

These methods of testing the metal content are expensive, even in my home country New Zealand, and in my opinion would never prove categorically that any bronze was genuinely from a Han or earlier period. As can be seen from the variances of the lead content on one ding, from traces to 43.91%, it would be impossible to arrive at any rational conclusions from such diverging results.

I made further inquiries as to the reasons for such discrepancies and there appear to be three distinct possible reasons for these variations:
1. Samples taken by electric drill for SEM testing can be contaminated by a phenomenon known in the industry as "lead smear". Curiously, it does not affect "wet testing", presumably because only the surface particles are smeared.
2. As the copper and tin has a higher melting point than lead, they harden first on the outside, forcing the lead particles (which do not alloy, but sit as globules) to the inside.

3. The copper, tin and lead, hardening at different temperatures, also flow unequally through the mould, so the alloy mix on one side of a vessel, may differ from that on another part of the same piece.

Using the SEM, we were able to photograph a lead globule suspended in the copper/tin alloy (Fig. 8).

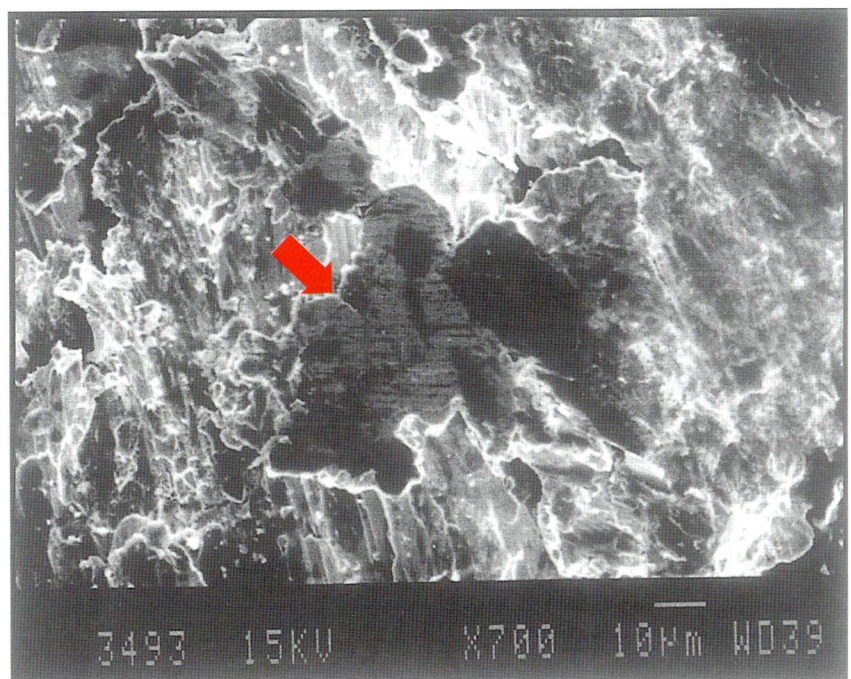

Fig.8 Photomicrograph Showing Lead Globule in Suspension

What these analyses did confirm, was the relatively high levels of lead used in many ancient Chinese bronzes, totally at variance with the traditional Chinese percentages, as referred to previously in Table 2.

Also to be noted from the SEM analysis, is the total absence of tin in the spear head (G), a feature of some bronze weapons especially, which has been noted by some earlier authors. This spear head is not bronze, but a mixture of copper and lead, the latter element in globular form.

There are some elements, if present in quantities of 1% or more, that may suggest that a bronze is of recent manufacture. I list a few that I think may be relevant:

1. Manganese   2. Silicon
3. Nickel   4. Zinc
5. Arsenic   6. Cadmium

Manganese and silicon are components of "silicon bronze", and silicon is a modern additive, which, like lead, reduces the melting point of copper. Nickel, zinc and arsenic may appear in small quantities in ancient Chinese bronzes, but if the percentage of any of them exceeded 1%, one would have to be on the alert that the item concerned was modern. Cadmium was not discovered until the 19th century.

Some of these elements may have been used in a modern repair, or (like cadmium) perhaps used in new gold or silver repair or inlay, so that possibility may also need to be considered.

Another possible aspect to be considered, for anyone fortunate to have access to x-ray diffraction equipment, is the detection of copper nitrate in the corrosion. Many of the better fake green patinas have been created by a nitric acid-based formula, which leaves copper nitrate in the patina; something which does not occur naturally. Again, the possibility exists that a new patina was applied over a repair, or a non-nitric acid based formula was used, so the presence or absence of copper nitrate, by itself, will not prove conclusively that a bronze is genuine or fake.

Latterly, because of their non-destructive nature, there has been an increasing tendency to use surface analytical techniques, such as PIXE (particle induced x-ray emissions) to attempt to authenticate ancient Chinese bronzes. However, PIXE provides only compositional analysis of the surface tested, and until such time as we have published comparative data from authenticated similar examples, PIXE results are in my opinion not of much assistance.

My own opinion, based on my reading of numbers of authors' analyses of the metal content, is that there are no scientific testing procedures known to us at the present time, based on metallurgical analysis of the base metals, that will positively authenticate a Chinese bronze as being Han or earlier.

However, while warning bells will ring if there is a total absence of lead, even that will not be conclusive, for as Gettens recorded (The Freer Chinese Bronzes, Vol. 2, Technical Studies, 1969) several bronze vessels among his test sample had no lead content.

In fact, the only conclusion to be drawn for the present, is the inconclusiveness of metallurgical analysis.

CHAPTER 7
X-RAY ANALYSIS

X-ray analysis, or radiography, is, in my experience, the least expensive and, (if one wishes to gain some degree of certainty that the bronze in question is genuine), potentially the most helpful of any of the scientific procedures that I have seen. I have used the x-ray facilities of Materials and Testing Laboratories Ltd, an Auckland company, more used to testing welders for their annual practising certificates, or pipe joins for welds, than for authenticating ancient Chinese bronzes. Each x-ray costs only between $US12 and $US30 per shot, depending on the size of the film, and the time taken to shoot and develop it.

X-ray analysis may show any or all of the following positive features of authentication:

7.1 The Presence of Spacers (Chaplets)
In my experience, most, but not all ancient Chinese bronze vessels have had spacers used in their fabrication, necessary to keep the mould walls to an even thickness.

The lid of the ding (B on the cover), (Fig. 9) shows a radiating band of spacers, at regular intervals from 10 o'clock to 5.30 o'clock. The spacers on the other side, with the exception of one at 8 o'clock, have melted and fused with the pour, indicating that the left hand side was probably poured first. Note also the variations in darkness of the x-ray, indicating varying thicknesses of the lid, and the multitude of blemishes and black spots, caused perhaps by impurities, but more commonly by air bubbles.

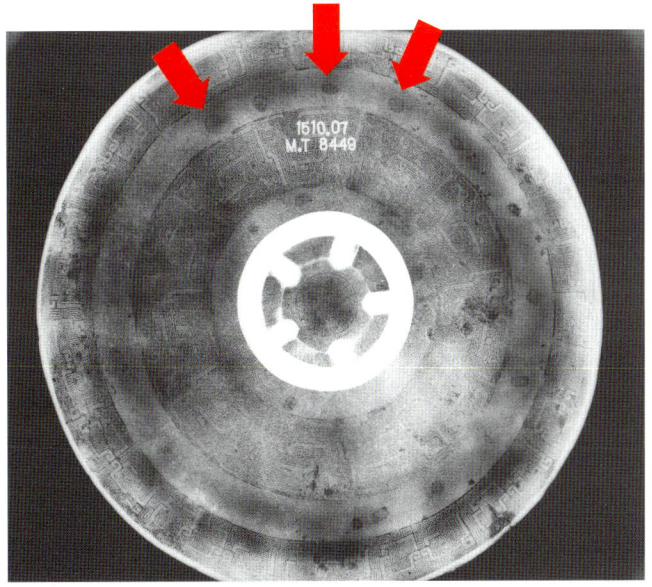

Fig.9 X-ray of Ding Lid (B on the Cover)

7.2 Ancient Repairs

The lidded hu vase (F on the cover), has an ancient repair (Fig. 10) disclosed by x-ray, which I cannot see even with a 20 power magnifying glass. Note the mass of air bubbles in the primitive, but very effective, weld.

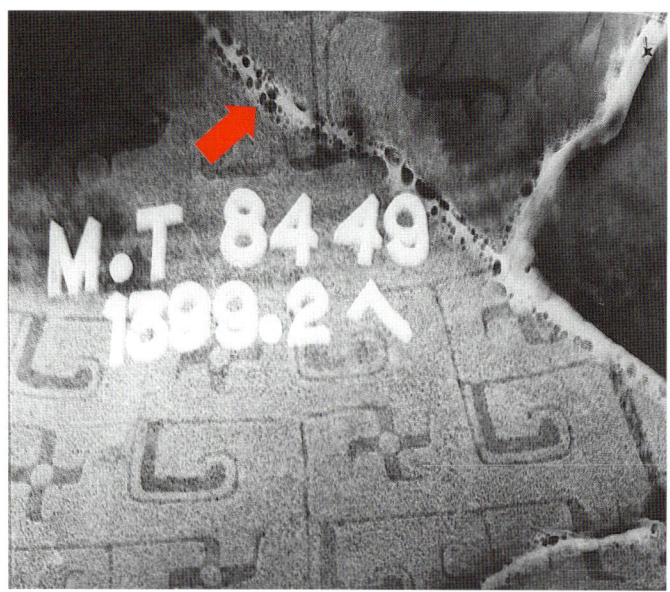

Fig.10 Ancient Repair on a Hu Vase (F on the Cover)

7.3 Modern Repairs

As I have stated previously, the vast majority of genuine bronzes on the market today have sustained some degree of damage, resulting in repair. The most extensive repair that I have encountered, other than the ding illustrated later (Fig.20), is the underside of another lidded ding (Fig.11). The workmanship and re-patination is simply extraordinary, and, but for the detached leg, I would probably never have known of the repair. Note the multitude of metal pins holding the broken pieces in place.

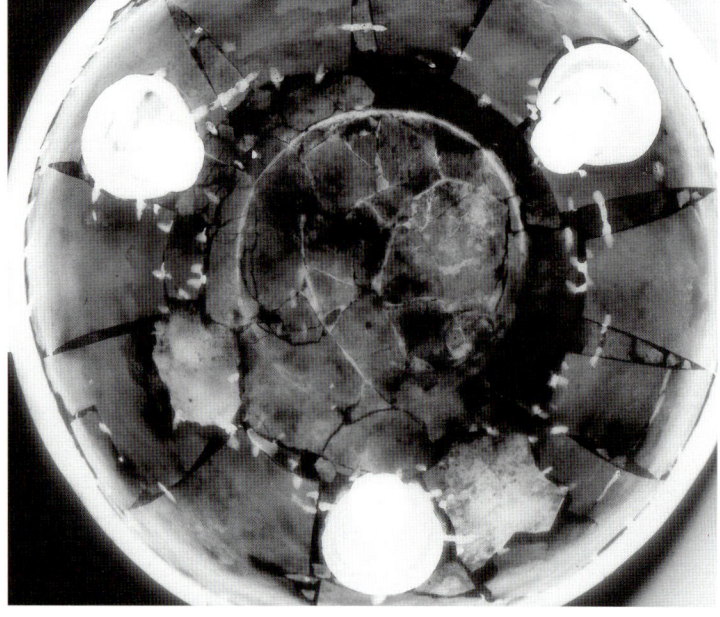

Fig.11 Repaired Base of Lidded Ding as Revealed by X-ray

7.4 Ancient Mould Lines & Casting Marks

On some ancient bronzes it is not possible to visually see the ancient sectional mould lines, or casting marks (vents, sprues etc), either because of the quality of finishing, or more usually, because of the heavy encrustation of corrosion. The casting sprue on a ding (Fig. 74b) shows plainly on the x-ray (arrowed Fig. 12).

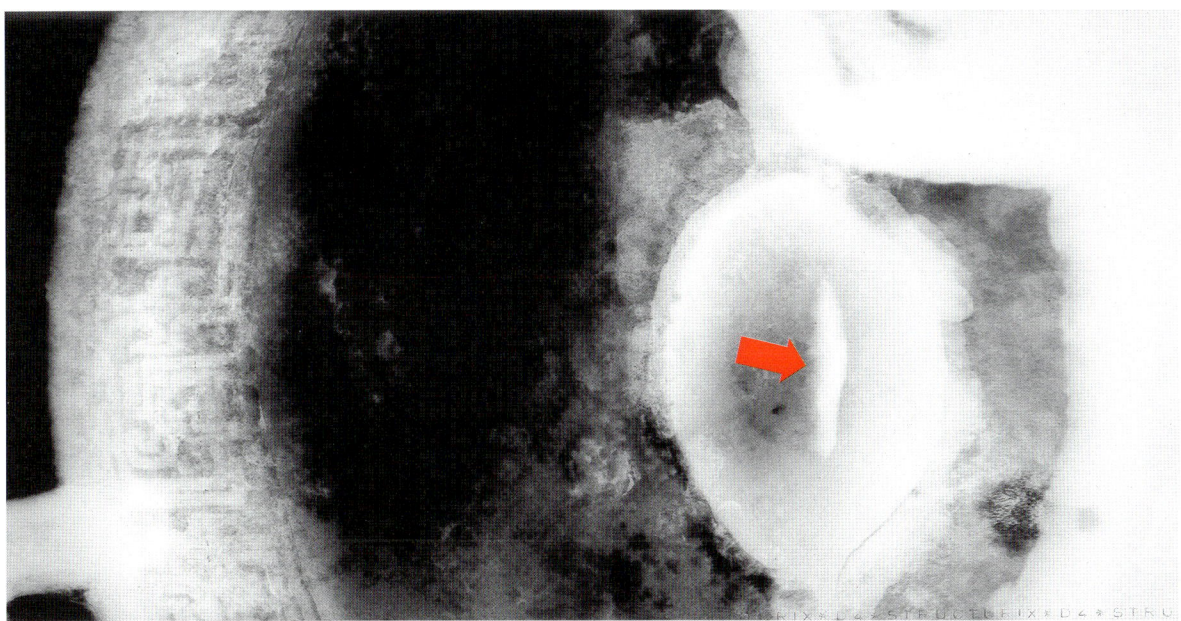

Fig. 12 Ancient Sprue Mark Revealed by X-ray

7.5 Defects, Blemishes & Air Bubbles

Arguably the most prevalent feature of x-rays of all of these ancient bronzes, are the defects, blemishes and air bubbles. Frequently, there are seepages between the mould edges, resulting in denser areas of bronze, or mould edges shifted in the pour, causing designs to be out of alignment, or as Fig.69 shows, totally out of round.

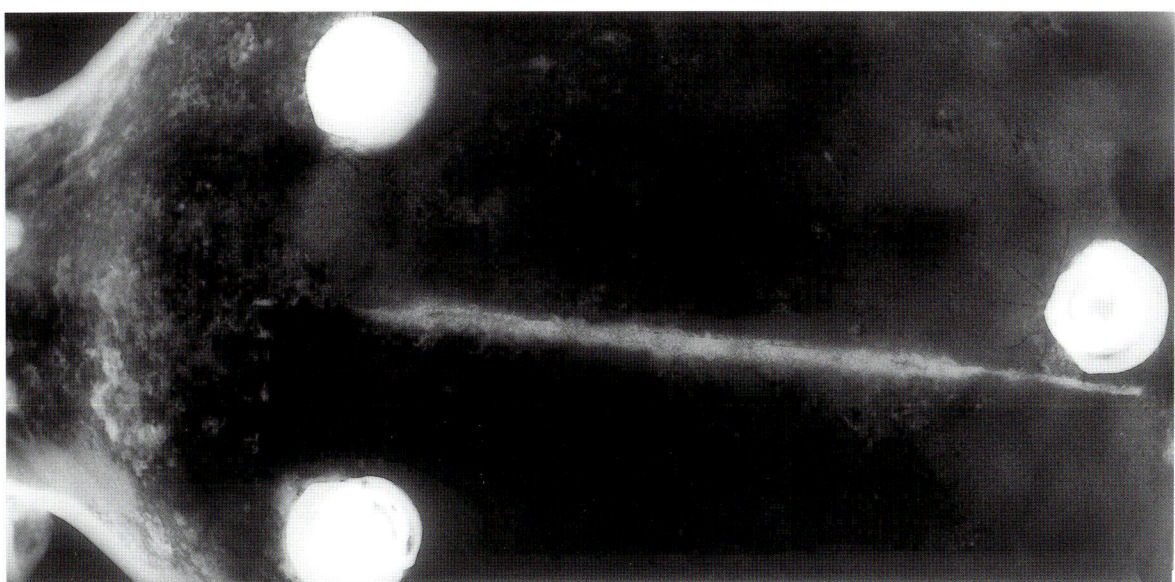

Fig. 13 Base of a Spring & Autumn Period Yi Wine Vessel (Fig. 147)

Comparison of the x-ray of the Spring and Autumn yi wine vessel (Fig.13), with that of a modern reproduction (Fig.14), shows immediately the difference. The modern yi, in addition to having pin holes (arrowed) for lost wax (or lost foam) casting, has virtually none of the imperfections of its earlier counterpart.

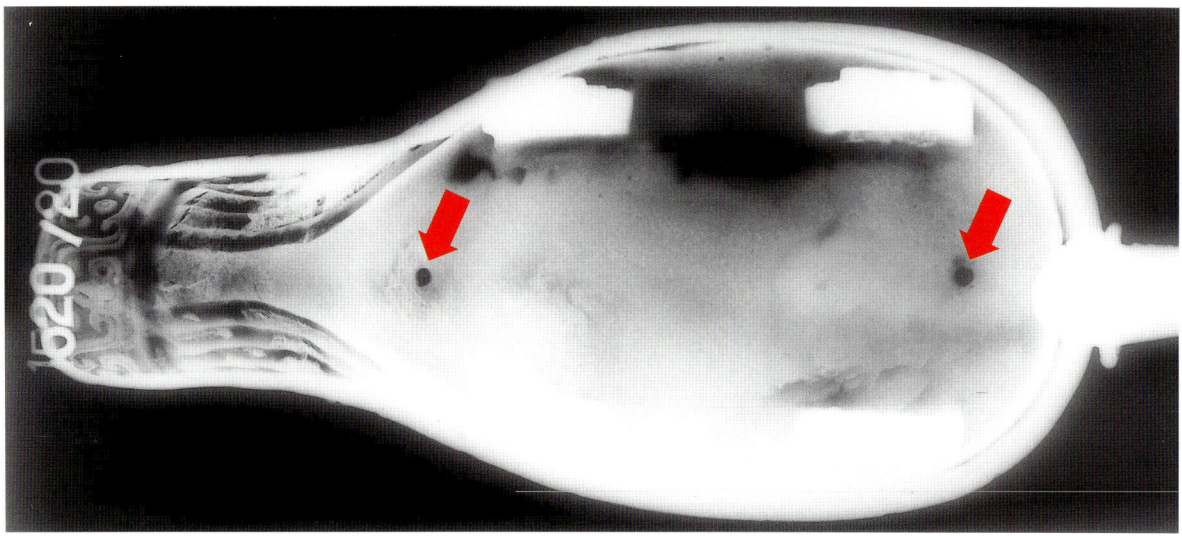

Fig. 14 X-ray of a Modern Fake Yi Wine Vessel

7.6 Clay Cores

Clay cores are a recurring feature of ancient Chinese bronze technology, especially during the Zhou dynasty. They are to be found occasionally attached to bases of wine jars (Fig.16), as cores of Buddhas (post Han dynasty), inside attached lugs or added features (eg. bird finials etc), and especially, inside both cast and applied legs of tripod dings (Fig.15). Usually the presence of the core will be detected visually, but in some cases, the clay core may be confirmed only by x-ray.

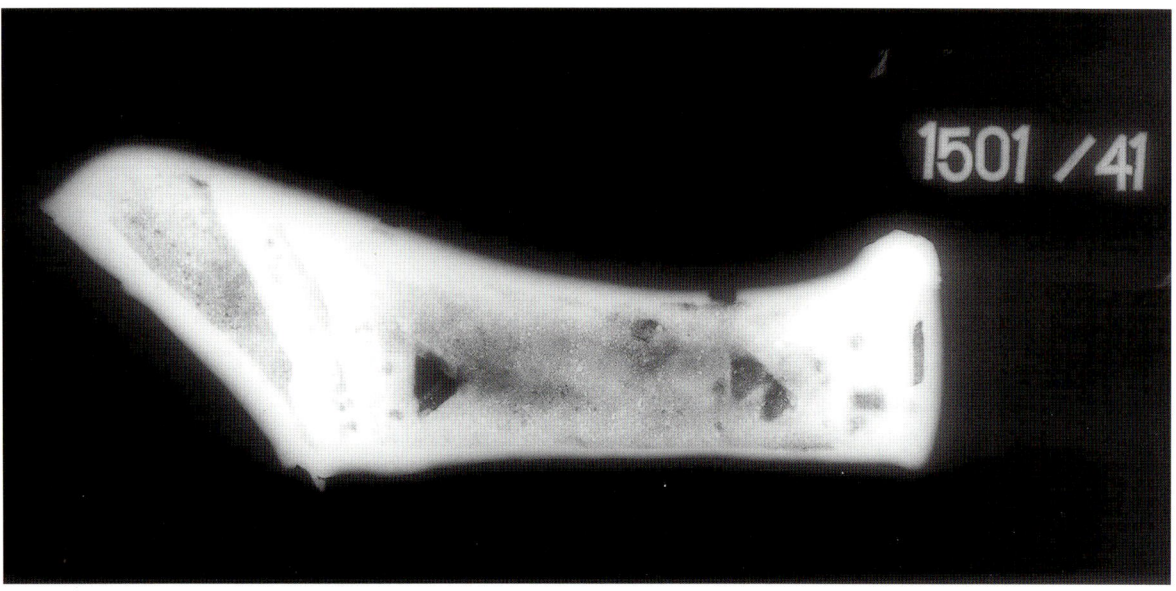

Fig. 15 X-ray of Ding Leg Revealing Clay Core

CHAPTER 8
THERMOLUMINESCENCE & CARBON 14 DATING

Thermoluminescence and carbon 14 dating, both potentially can provide some assurance that a bronze article is an antique; ie. not new. But the use of such testing procedures must be done with some caution, for as I will illustrate, the base materials on which these tests rely, are open to natural distortion or, in some cases, outright fabrication.

8.1 Thermoluminescence
Thermoluminescence (TL) testing will not by itself date any bronze, but it may give some assurances as to the age of a bronze. In a ceramic, any geological thermoluminescence will be eliminated once it is fired, allowing it to build up again at a constant rate. This accumulation of TL energy can be measured, so that the greater the readings of thermoluminescence, the longer the time period since it was last hot; over say 500 degrees Celsius.

A number of these ancient bronze vessels, as I have previously mentioned, have fired clay cores; particularly on the bases, or inside any attached legs or lugs.

Fig. 16 Fired Clay Core on the Base of a Lidded Hu Vase (F on the Cover)

Samples of the clay core on the base of a lidded hu vase, which stylistically dates to the Warring States period (2300 to 2500 years old), were sent to the University Of Wollongong in Australia, for TL testing. The TL test results came back as 2000 years old, supporting a description as "consistent with the dating of the vessel", even though they may have been up to 500 years different from the actual date of manufacture. TL tests are not 100% accurate, and in any event will be distorted by heating (in a fire, as the sooty base of this hu indicates, or perhaps by gas brazing during repair), or by x-rays (perhaps during baggage or postal inspection). In Asia, in particular, the TL tests may also be subject to abuse by corrupt laboratories and/or their staff.

To illustrate this last point, I secretly took some photos of a group of Han dynasty (206BC to 220AD) pottery horses undergoing restoration in a warehouse in China (Fig.17).

Fig.17 Han Dynasty Pottery Horses in the Process of Restoration

Restoration is to be expected in the case of these horses, as almost every one has sustained some degree of damage, and not all broken pieces are recovered, as can be seen by the repairs to the brown horse. But what is alarming, are the paper labels applied to the pale green horse, awaiting its final coat of glaze, indicating where the TL tester is to drill in order to get genuine readings (Fig.18).

I know of one U.S. dealer, who because of experiences like this, will not accept any Asian originating TL test certificate. There are to my knowledge only two TL test facilities in Hong Kong, (and one agency), and these labels indicate that the samples of at least one of them are not independently taken. Furthermore, the Singapore branch of one TL testing Company was allegedly closed, because its agent was taking bribes, and the Hong Kong agent dismissed for similar indiscretions. In the meantime, who but the agent knows how many faked TL certificates are in existence, just from these two?

Fig. 18 Paper Labels Indicating Drill Sites for TL Testing

Not all such largely genuine antique pottery items are just missing a few pieces, like the brown horse. Take the Han dynasty dog (Fig. 19), which has been entirely fabricated from unrelated Han pottery pieces, perhaps from a broken jar or stove.

Fig.19 Fabricated Han Dynasty Pottery Dog

It is not difficult for today's copyists to insert a genuine pottery core, or part of one, into an ancient bronze, and I have been told of one instance where this has been detected. It is also relatively easy to get a TL test done using one's own samples, or to simply reproduce (even with a colour photocopier) a genuine appearing test certificate.

Best defence is to use a reputable laboratory, like Wollongong University, who will state on their certificate that the samples were provided, if they did not independently take them themselves. Watch also for any certificate that states that the samples showed differing clays.

The current cost of a basic TL test at Wollongong University is $AUD220 ($US120).

Just prior to this book going to the printers, I arranged for thermoluminescence testing of samples from the cores of a further three ancient bronze vessels and 18 pottery figures, the latter ranging in date from the Han to the Ming dynasties. This brought to five, the number of core samples from ancient bronzes, which I have had thermoluminescence tested by Wollongong University.

The results, from a dating perspective, were disappointing (Table 4).

Table 4 Thermoluminescence Dating of Five Samples			
Description	**Fig. Ref.**	**Suggested Age**	**TL Test Age**
Spade Coin	160	2200 to 2400	280
Lidded Hu Vase	113	2300 to 2500	2000
Gui	102	2300 to 2500	2100
Lidded Ding	79	2300 to 2500	2000
Ding	70	2800 to 3000	2300

With reference to Table 4, the Fig. Ref. refers to the illustration number in this book, and the suggested age and TL test age are in years before present. Every TL test age suggested a dating younger than is suggested by the shape and decoration of the piece tested.

In an e-mail communication to me, David Price from Wollongong University advised in respect of the gui, *"The result is an age of 2100 years BP which, whilst on the young side, is as close needs be to show authenticity given all of the uncertainties associated with authenticity testing i.e., the burial environment, exact potassium level of the core, radioactive properties of the bronze itself, small sample etc."*

In a following communication, he expanded on his initial comments, stating

"Generally the results are fairly close but this depends on the piece under test. What can be said is that if the piece stylistically belongs to a given period and the TL result is reasonably close, i.e., definitely not suggestive of a recent copy (100, 40 years or modern) then the piece is genuine. It may be that bronzes have a few additional unknowns as compared to pottery. For example the casting core material is scraped from close to the bronze metal itself and this may deliver a very different radiation dose to the core material than the actual core itself; which is, of course, the only thing the TL dosimetry measurements can be made upon in the lab."

In fairness to David Price and Wollongong University, for whom I have the highest respect, it should be made clear that these relatively abundant bronze vessels are only a recent phenonemon. As more and more are made available for TL testing, and in my experience only a small percentage have TL testable cores in any event, then perhaps the TL measurements for bronzes may require reassessment.

8.2 Carbon 14 Dating

All living organisms contain small quantities of the radioactive isotope 14C, which originates from the atmosphere. Once the organism is dead, no further radioactive material is absorbed and the radioactive carbon atoms slowly decay, enabling measurement of the age of the organism by accelerator mass spectrometry. In New Zealand, this technology is available through Rafter Radiocarbon Laboratory in Lower Hutt, but owing to the high cost ($NZ900 or $US400 per sample), I have not yet had occasion to use it.

Carbon 14 dating is a potentially useful confirmative test of the age of carbonaceous materials which are found in, or attaching to, ancient Chinese bronzes.

Some examples:
1. The remains of a lacquer scabbard or the binding on a sword, or the wooden box in which it was once stored.
2. The remains of fat or soot on the underside of a bronze cooking vessel, especially the dings.
3. The remains of food in a pot, or charcoal in an incense burner.
4. Traces of wood, binding, tree roots, fabric etc embedded in the corrosion.

However, it must be remembered that the date shown will not necessarily be the age of the bronze, but perhaps the age of the tree from whence the wood came, or the tree root when it died. Furthermore, the date will not be more accurate than plus or minus 50 years, and, owing to the progressive pollution of the atmosphere from the burning of fossil fuels, it is of no assistance in dating organisms after 1700AD.

But a tree root dated to say 700 years embedded in the corrosion, is going to be pretty difficult to fake, and the presence of such an item, should at least confirm that the bronze in question is not a modern fake.

CHAPTER 9

HIGH POWER MICROSCOPY & DIGITAL SCANNING

Close-up inspection of an allegedly ancient bronze, either by high power microscopy or high resolution digital scanning, may provide confirmation that the piece is or is not genuine. But extreme caution is needed. Take the bronze ding, which I surreptitiously photographed in the course of repair (Fig. 20).

Fig.20 Warring States Bronze Ding in the Course of Repair

This ding, as can be seen from the photograph, is being reconstructed from a mass of broken parts. Sections are missing, including one lug which must be recast, and the repair appears to use a lead-based solder, the remains of which will be required to be ground off. This will undoubtedly leave a modern "tool signature" visible under a microscope; but only if the person using the microscope examines a repaired section.

The evidence of lathe turning marks on the pommel of the sword (Fig. 201c), was visible under a 20 power eyeglass, proving this sword to be a modern fake. (Fig.21). The inset photo of a genuine Warring States sword pommel, from the sword (Fig. 195a) shows the difference between the two. Note the lines across the grooves, on the right hand ancient sword, almost like "milling" marks on a coin, presumably to give the now missing inlay something to bind to.

Care must also be taken to ensure that file or wire brush marks, in particular, whether rotary or in straight lines, are not mistaken as evidence of modern fabrication;

when in fact they occurred during cleaning of an ancient burial bronze, of the deposits of soil and corrosion. Or, in the case of an edged weapon, were made during ancient sharpening.

Fake   **Genuine**

Fig. 21 Modern Lathe Tool Signature on a Fake Sword

Another possibility to consider, if one is examining the corrosion deposits under either method, is that the ancient bronze in question has not been artificially repatinated, either to improve its appearance, or, more usually, to conceal a recent repair. Occasionally, a new or non-original pommel may be added to an old sword.

I personally prefer the high resolution close-up digital scanning, as it enables the viewer to scan quite large areas of the surface, not just one small area under a microscope. Using this method, I have been able to find other confirmations of antiquity; eg ancient hole repairs, traces of fabric etc (Fig.22 & 23).

Fig.22 Ancient Hole Repair   **Fig.23 Traces of Fabric in the Corrosion**

The hole repair (Fig.22) was on the base of the lidded hu vase (F on the cover), while the fabric was found on the inside of the lid of the gui (Fig.106).

CHAPTER 10

PATINATION & CORROSION

The natural patination of bronze, which occurs over centuries of burial, comes from within the bronze, while artificially induced chemical patination must of necessity be on the surface. Visually it is often very difficult to distinguish a modern patina from the genuine ancient original, and in the case of re-patination after repair, it is often almost impossible to confirm a dating one way or the other.

There is one simple test that can sometimes confirm either a modern patina or re-patination. Take a solvent like acetone (I use nail polish remover), and with a cloth or swab, wipe a small section of the green patina. If the green comes off, you will almost undoubtedly have a modern patina, perhaps applied to an ancient bronze. It must be noted that this only works on the cheapest and most basic patinas. On well patinated modern copies, the patina will not wipe off.

Another pointer to look for, as it is found on numerous poor quality fake bronzes, is a cerussite (grey/white) patina which flakes off when scratched. Other fakes (or new patination on an old bronze) may simply have a green paint applied. A more expensive patination process is to grind up quantities of the corroded materials (malachite, cuprite and azurite) and apply them with glue (Fig. 24). Many modern paints and glues will fluoresce under exposure to ultra-violet light. However, neither solvents nor ultra-violet light will necessarily expose every falsely applied patinas; (eg. if animal glues have been used).

Fig. 24 Ground Malachite Used to Conceal a Modern Repair

An area of damage around one of the ring handles on the fanghu vase (C on the cover), once repaired has been re-patinated using ground malachite particles. Note the areas of raised patina, immediately below and to either side, of the loop. (Fig, 24). The areas of repair are clearly shown in the x-ray (Fig. 25). Note again, the spacers on this vase, also exposed by x-ray.

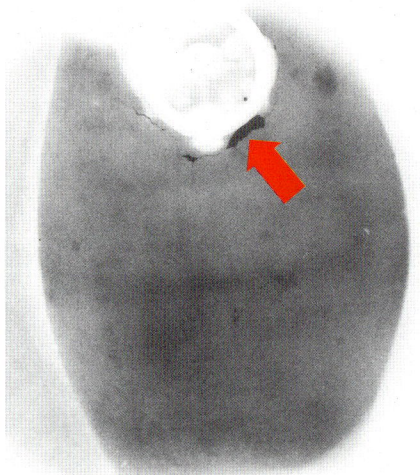

Fig. 25   X-ray of the Repatinated Area Showing Areas of Repair

Gettens also refers to other materials used in false patination, including emerald green (or Paris green or copper aceto-arsenite), Prussian blue (a dye), artificial ultramarine, smalt (a cobalt-based powdered glass) and others. Some of these may be identified by high power microscopy or pigment analysis, but as they may also have been used in re-patination, their identification alone may not prove conclusively that the bronze in question is, or is not, a genuine antiquity.

The most commonly encountered natural patinas, formed by corrosion of the bronze alloys, comes in four distinct colours. These are:

(a) Cuprite.
This is a reddish colour, often found in conjunction with the green

Fig. 26 Red Cuprite

(b) Malachite

This is the greenish colour which is to be found on most corroded bronzes. Depending on the conditions and length of burial, the malachite corrosion can vary from a relatively light coating (Fig 27), taken from the ding (Fig.70) to a heavy encrustation, (Fig.28), taken from the gui (Fig.33). It is also the most commonly faked colour of all patinas.

Fig. 27 Green Malachite

Fig. 28 Green Malachite

In some circumstances the malachite corrosion forms distinct bubbles, not dissimilar to burnt paint, and this phenomena is referred to as botryoidal malachite. In my experience, it is one of the surest confirmations of antiquity, as to date I have not seen it on any fake bronze. Unfortunately, it is only to be found on a relatively small percentage of ancient Chinese bronzes.

Fig. 29 Botryoidal Malachite

(c) Cerussite

This is the lead-based corrosion, which usually manifests itself in an unappealing grey-white colour, and will often be found in conjunction with cuprite corrosion. Note also the spacer (arrowed) showing in this close-up of the lid of the lidded bowl (Fig.110).

Fig. 30 Cerussite

(d) Azurite

This is the deep blue coloured corrosion, most commonly found on the inside of lids and bodies, or underneath the raised foot of vessels; presumably where it was better protected from damp. Azurite is usually accompanied by malachite corrosion, and is, in my experience, a usually reliable sign of antiquity. I have seen fake azurite patination, but to date these have been very thin, and not of the intense blue colour that genuine azurite patinas usually are.

Fig.31 Azurite

(e) Tin Oxide

This is usually found on bronzes with relatively high tin content, especially the edges of swords and daggers. Research at the National Palace Museum in Taipei suggests that on more elaborate swords, a higher tin content edge was separately cast to each side of the central shaft. This enabled the swords to be better sharpened, and to hold a sharper edge, as well as strengthening the whole sword by the lamination.

The x-ray which I took of one Warring States sword (x-ray not shown), did not show any laminated edges, although there was significant evidence of tin oxide corrosion, indicated by brittle and crumbling edges (Fig. 32). I suspect that the ancient bronze casters simply cooled the outside edges first, causing the tin (which hardens before the lead) to concentrate on the extremities. This however must remain as speculation, until such time as someone interested enough in the subject, "wet tests" the alloy contents of both the edges and the central spine.

Fig. 32 Tin Oxide

The range of genuine patinas found is quite remarkable, making authentication by patina comparison, in some cases, extremely difficult. Collectors should remember that the circumstances of burial varied dramatically. Some bronzes were buried in vaults, others in arid regions of China, largely protected from soil and water corrosion. Many were buried in tombs on less arable, but better draining, hillsides, possibly accounting for the good state of preservation of many bronzes found today. Other bronzes were not so fortunate, perhaps being buried in wetlands, in salt marshes, or even next to or on top of the deceased.

As an example of extreme corrosion, and to demonstrate why I am vehemently opposed to those academics who prefer to leave these ancient bronzes in the ground until such time as they can get around to unearthing them, I have illustrated the gui of Fig.33.

Fig. 33 An Extremely Corroded Western Zhou Gui

Surely it is better to recover these fragile bronzes now, at the expense of the possible loss of their archaeological history, than to risk losing them altogether to corrosion?

Another point for readers to consider is the possibility that a fake was made in the centuries subsequent to the original time of manufacture. Certainly, ancient Chinese bronzes were copied during the Song dynasty (960 to 1279AD), and possibly as early as the Han dynasty. A number of fakes were produced subsequently, notably in the Ming dynasty and the early 20th century. Some are composites of fake and genuine parts, while others are assemblages of various, but unrelated, genuine bronze pieces. Many of the bronzes available today have been repaired, had parts recast, or bear no relationship to what they originally looked like.

And finally, some genuine ancient bronzes have been cleaned, even to look like polished brass, thus making authentication especially difficult.

CHAPTER 11

POSITIVE VISUAL CONSIDERATIONS IN AUTHENTICATION

In my previous discussions on methods of authentication, I have briefly touched on a number of visual aspects which can help in authenticating the age of a Chinese bronze. At the risk of repeating myself, I now wish to expand upon these, by illustration where possible. Readers must again remember, that these indicators of age may have been faked, so they must remain alert to that possibility.

11.1 Seams & Mould Joins

The majority of Chinese bronzes made before the Han dynasty were cast in sectional moulds, and evidence of these moulds, which may in some cases have been cleaned up in post-cast finishing, will not usually be removed in total.

Fig. 34 Mould Line on a Western Zhou Ding

The mould line, (Fig. 34) running vertically above the leg, separates the panels of leiwen decoration. Note that the left hand panel is slightly lower than that on the right, and these slipped or misaligned panels are a recurring feature of genuine ancient bronzes. The legs on this ding have been separately cast with clay cores, and attached to the body in a separate process.

The misalignment of mould joins is even more apparent on the hu vase (Fig. 35) (I on the cover).

Fig. 35 Misaligned Mould Join on a Hu Vase

Occasionally, the mould itself would crack, causing the molten bronze to run into the cracks, as can be seen in the x-ray of a lidded gui (Fig.36). Note also the two ancient spacers, and at four o'clock, the ancient repair.

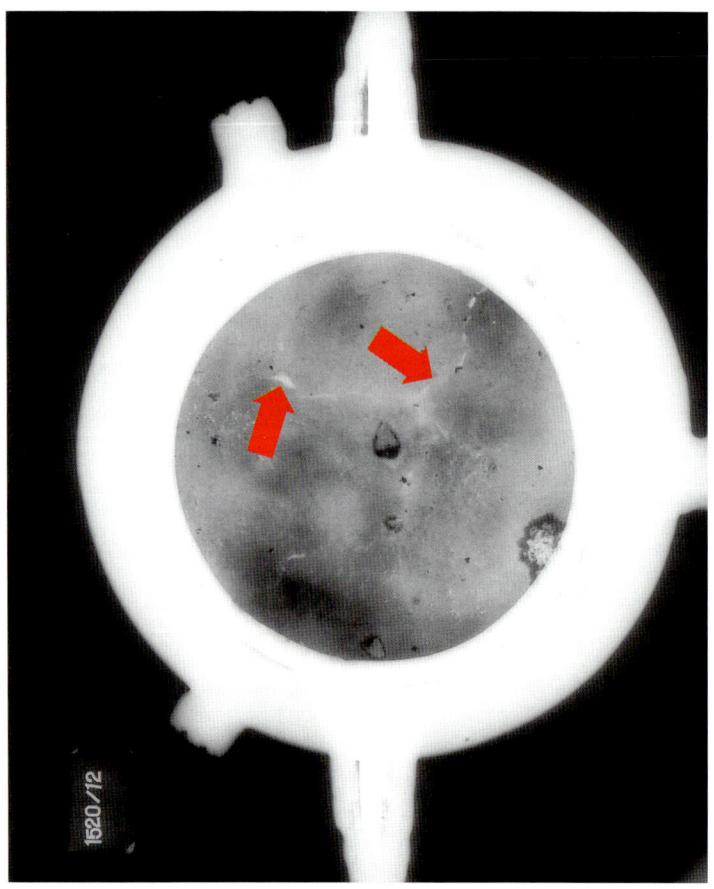

Fig. 36 Broken Mould Lines as Seen by X-ray

Triangular or circular mould lines are a recurring feature of the undersides of ancient bronze dings, as is the sooty black base where the ding has been used over a fire (Fig.37).

Fig. 37 Circular Mould Lines on the Underside of a Large Eastern Zhou Ding

11.2 Sprue & Vent Marks

In my experience it is uncommon to find the original sprue marks where the bronze was poured, as they seem usually to have been erased in post-cast finishing. The legs of the ding (Fig.67) have been used as the sprue, this fact evidenced by the concave centre of the leg, where the bronze has contracted on cooling. In this instance, the legs have not been applied later, but are solid cast as part of the body.

Fig. 38 Base of Ding Leg Showing Sprue Mark

There may be some debate as to the reason for the triangular holes in the foot rim of the hu vase (I on the cover), but because the spacers in the top are square (Fig.2), I believe that these are vent holes to allow gas to escape during the pour (Fig. 39).

Fig. 39 Vent Marks in the Foot Rim of a Hu Vase

11.3 Clay Cores

I have seen only one fake bronze with clay cores, either in legs, lugs, bases or lids, so their presence to date has been a reassuring confirmation of antiquity. I illustrate two more genuine examples, the first from the badly corroded Western Zhou gui (Fig.33), the second from the magnificent Western Han hu vase (Fig.116). The remains of the core was also present in the lid of this vase.

Fig. 40 Base of Western Zhou Gui   Fig. 41 Base of Western Han Hu Vase

11.4 Spacers

I have illustrated a number of vessels showing the spacers used to keep the mould sides apart. Their presence has been widely publicised in at least one Chinese art magazine, and although I have yet to see any in the fakes which I have handled, I would not be surprised if they have been incorporated in recent copies.

11.5 Air Bubbles & Variations In The Thickness

These traditional defects of ancient casting technology can unfortunately only be seen by x-ray, but they pose a formidable problem for today's copyists to replicate.

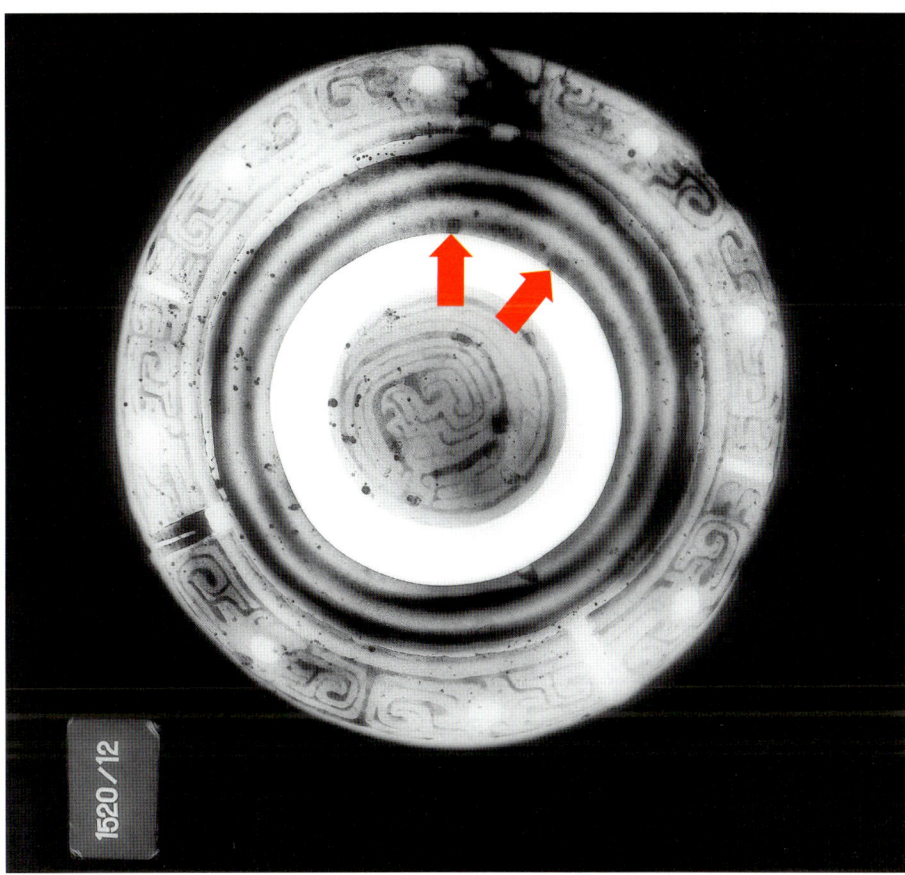

Fig. 42 Air Bubbles & Variations in Thickness as Seen by X-ray

The x-ray, of the gui lid (Fig.106), shows dense areas as white, thin areas and air bubbles as black. Note the variations in thickness, and again the presence of two visible (in this case square) spacers (arrowed).

11.6 Quality Of The Decoration

Such is the high quality of some of today's bronze casting, that the quality of decoration is seldom of any guide to a piece's age. However, occasionally one will come across an exceptional bronze, where the chances of fabrication are unlikely. Such is the decoration on the lidded hu vase (F on the cover). Note the remains of inlaid copper wire, under the eye and down the leg of the right hand bird (Fig. 43).

Fig. 43 Top Quality Inlaid Decoration on an Eastern Zhou Hu Vase

11.7 Attachments

Bronze was sometimes used for attachment to another metal, such as iron, or material, such as jade or wood. Such pieces may assist in confirming or otherwise, the antiquity of the bronze. For example, a Western Han bronze sword handle (Fig. 44), which contains pieces of the original, but now badly rusted iron blade.

Fig. 44 Western Han Bronze Sword Handle

Another Western Han sword handle (Fig. 45) has traces of the original binding embedded in the corrosion.

Fig. 45 Original Binding in the Corrosion of a Sword Handle

Binding is not restricted to sword handles, but is occasionally seen on the inside or outside of pole arm weapons, such as spear or axe heads. The wooden pole ends must have been wrapped in binding and the spear or axe head rammed onto the bound head, and then strapped to attach it. Such indicators of age are helpful, particularly given the fact that these handles are being reproduced today.

Among the many chattels that were buried with the departed to accompany him or her in the afterlife, were their tools and weapons, many of which had wooden shafts, some of which have been partially preserved (Fig. 46). These spear heads, which date to the Warring States period, are illustrated Fig.187.

Fig. 46 Remains of Wood Shafts in Spear Heads

I have also seen wood and lacquer boxes holding swords, lacquer scabbards, also for swords, as were the jade guards and slides on bronze or bronze and iron bladed swords.

11.8 Debris In The Corrosion

In my experience, far and away the most positive indicator of antiquity, is the presence of carbonaceous debris in the corrosion. This can range from the fibrous material on the side of the fanghu vase (C on the cover), to the wood embedded in the side of a sword blade (Fig.201b) or the silk (or other) fabric that was often draped over or around these vessels and implements.

Fig. 47 Fibres on a Fanghu Vase

Fig 48 Wood on a Sword Blade

The incense burner (Fig. 155), obviously sat on a piece of timber, parts of which have attached itself in the corrosion.

Fig. 49 Wood Attaching to a Han Incense Burner

Fig. 50 Binding on a Shang Spear Head

Woven binding, and fabric, is an oft-recurring indicator of age, as can be seen on the close-up of a Shang dynasty spear head. (Fig. 50). Note also the dirt, and the good azurite and malachite patina.

11.9 Dirt & Tree Or Plant Roots

Most of the modern fakes have dirt rubbed into them, so the presence of dirt may not be overly helpful. Much of China's soil is a very heavy clay, which after centuries of compaction, is difficult to remove, and often results in the bronze piece getting scratched, by the over-zealous farm workers who find them. Such a piece is the Spring and Autumn period he wine vessel (Fig. 112), the base of which is illustrated (Fig. 51). Note the tree roots running through the clay. Often the tree roots will be embedded in the corrosion.

Fig. 51 Dirt & Tree Roots on a Spring & Autumn He Wine Vessel

11.10 Ancient & Modern Repairs

Both the ancient and modern repairs could sometimes be so skilful that their presence can only be found by x-ray examination. At other times, the repair obviously wasn't that important, as in the case of the sword handle (Fig. 52), which would originally have been covered by a cord binding. The modern day repair to the Warring States period spear head (Fig. 53), is almost visually undetectable.

Fig. 52 Old Repair **Fig. 53 Modern Repair**

The lid of a ding (Fig. 54), under x-ray, shows a long repaired crack, which I believe has been recently repaired. Readers wanting to check whether a repair is ancient or modern, should look under x-ray, for air bubbles in the ancient repaired cracks. Many of the modern day cracks or repairs are fixed with either lead solder or automotive panel-beaters' "bog". Remember, that most ancient Chinese bronzes have sustained some degree of damage and repair during their lifetime.

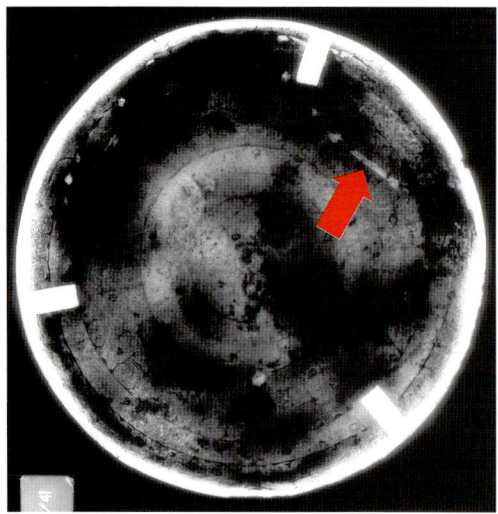

Fig. 54 Repaired Crack to Ding Lid Visible Under X-ray

11.11 "Frozen" Joints

The corrosion from centuries of burial, often left previously free-moving parts frozen in place, as in the case of the ring handle on the massive hu vase (A on the cover) (Fig. 55). Note the combined cuprite, azurite, cerussite and malachite corrosion around this ring handle, a combination which is very difficult to replicate. I have also seen these ring handles on modern fakes glued in place to simulate age, so caution is necessary. It is not uncommon to find genuine bronze crossbow mechanisms seized; also the cotter pins in bronze chariot axle hubs.

Fig. 55 "Frozen" Ring Handle on a Han Hu Vase

11.12 Wear & Missing Parts

Genuine wear is not likely to be something that the copyist will copy, so its presence can give some assurance of age. Take the Han or Warring States period horse bridle bit, the joints of which I have illustrated. (Fig. 56)

Fig. 56 Wear on a Han or Warring States Horse Bridle Bit

Another possible assurance of age, also obviously easily faked, is damage or missing parts. However, most bronze copyists tend to make perfect (as distinct from damaged) replicas, so a broken or missing part may indicate age. Having said that, I have seen a fake you wine vessel, minus its chains, presumably because they were too difficult to cast.

11.13 Variations In The Corrosion Or Patina

Most faked patina is relatively constant, whereas the genuine "centuries in the making" patina can vary quite markedly on one piece. This is better illustrated on what is admittedly a more extreme case (Fig.57), a Warring States period hu vase (I on the cover) which must have fallen on one side during burial. Readers should look for the mix of patina; cuprite, malachite, cerussite and azurite, not necessarily all present, but usually in combinations of two or more.

Fig. 57 Variations in Corrosion on Two Sides of a Warring States Hu

11.14 Water Or Wine Stains

Numbers of the wine and food vessels buried with the dead contained water or wine, or, in many instances, had ground water enter them after burial. These fluids often left water marks on the inside of the vessel, and especially where they are canted at an angle (because the bowl or ding etc has fallen over), have in my experience provided an encouraging assurance of antiquity; something I have also yet to see replicated on the fakes.

11.15 Other Possible Indicators Of Antiquity

There are a number of other indications of age, all unfortunately easily replicated, some of which I now mention;

(a) Trellis Lines On The Undersides

In my experience, admittedly on lesser quality bronzes, I have to date not come across the "cross hatch" or trellis pattern which appears on the bases of several of the Freer and other museum bronzes. Readers should however be alert to this.

(b) Inward Bending Rims

Several (but by no means all) of the vessels illustrated in this book, have an inward bending rim and/or foot rim. They were obviously cast this way, something I have not noted on modern copies.

(c) Cross-shaped Holes In Gu Wine Vessels

Many (but again not all) Shang dynasty and Western Zhou gu wine beakers have slotted or cross-shaped holes just above the narrowest section of the vessel. It is presumed that these supported a bracket which kept the moulds in place during firing. Examples are illustrated Fig. 97 and Fig.100.

(d) "Bald" Patches

This is another curious feature of some ancient bronzes. A vessel may be generally covered in corrosion, yet there can be "bald" areas where the bronze is like new.

(e) Hardened Slime

This is often found on the insides of sealed vessels, such as lidded hu, the dark coloured slime often dry and lifting like paint, sometimes even giving the appearance of a dried fungus growth.

(f) Rust Stains

Some bronzes (eg. Fig.145) came into contact with iron objects during burial, and the resulting orange rust stains are usually a positive sign of antiquity.

CHAPTER 12

INSCRIPTIONS & INLAID DESIGNS

Readers must appreciate that the presence of either inscriptions or inlaid designs adds appreciably to the value of the bronze in question. As a consequence, ancient bronzes are frequently embellished with recently added inscriptions or inlay, the authentication of which can be extremely difficult. The collector or dealer in bronzes must also contend with wholly fake bronzes, and reconstructed bronzes, either of which can have later added inlay or inscriptions. To add to the confusion, some ancient inlay work which has been degraded or lost, may have been restored in recent times.

There are, however, a few generalisations that can assist the collector or dealer in identifying whether or not the inscription or inlay is contemporary with the date of manufacture of the bronze.

The first step is to verify that the bronze is in fact ancient, and, preferably with x-ray or microscope, determine that it is not reconstructed. The approximate age may then be able to be determined from the shape and design.

12.1 Inscriptions

Inscriptions on bronzes from the Shang dynasty (pre-1122BC) will almost invariably be short in length, perhaps containing only the clan name or the name of the deceased. Those of the Zhou dynasty could be up to several dozen or more characters. Bronzes with long inscriptions seldom come from burial sites, but rather the hoards where they were buried or concealed at times of great internal strife. These long inscriptions were originally made to be read and admired, so they appeared on the ritual vessels used for ancestor worship, not burial. Most of the characters will be written in the ancient pictogram script. These characters will usually have been added in one of several ways:

(a) Casting in high relief. Unless the characters have been applied to a separately added panel, and this is unlikely, then they must have been done at the time the bronze vessel was cast; by carving the characters in reverse in the clay mould. So whatever the age of the bronze, the inscription should be contemporary with this. Such characters stand higher than the body on which they appear.

(b) Casting in low relief. In this case the characters are raised in high relief on the mould, but also in reverse, so that they give an indented inscription to the bronze body, similar to carving.

(c) Carving into the bronze after casting was completed. Such inscriptions have been much copied, and dating them is often extremely difficult (Fig. 58). This inscription is to be found on the rim of the massive Han dynasty hu vase, (A on the cover). According to one linguist whom I consulted, it reads "?? made this". I am intensely suspicious of it, although inscriptions like this of the period are not uncommon.

The inscription shown (Fig. 59) appears on an Eastern Zhou dagger axe.(Fig.182). I have yet to discover a reliable means of authenticating these inscriptions, but another Chinese linguist has declared this to be a forgery.

Fig.58 Carved Inscription on the Rim of a Hu Vase

Fig. 59 Carved Inscription on a Dagger Axe (Ge)

(d) Inlaid inscriptions. These may be done in copper, silver and even gold or semi-precious stones, but such are the activities of the forgers, that they should be viewed with considerable suspicion.

12.2 Inlaid Designs

The vast majority of inlaid designs on currently available Chinese bronzes have been added in recent times. The safest bet when first confronted with inlay is to view it with great suspicion. Most usual materials for inlay work, regardless of age, are copper, silver, gold and semi-precious stones, especially turquoise and malachite. Coloured glass, lacquer and other materials were also used.

The close-ups of the two sections of leiwen design (Fig. 60 and 61), appearing on the Eastern Zhou steamer (Fig.142) and the Western Zhou ding (Fig.67), would seem to be lacquer inlay. However, I have a nagging doubt that they may be soot deposits from the pieces being used for cooking purposes above a fire; a possibility that earlier authors do not appear to have considered.

Fig.60 Lacquer? Inlay on a Steamer   **Fig. 61 Lacquer? Inlay on a Ding**

Some inlay work is extremely detailed, as may be seen by the remaining copper wire inlay (Fig.62) of the hu vase (F on the cover). The design had first to be cut or cast into the bronze, before the fine copper wire was folded backwards and forwards to fill the design.

Fig. 62 Copper Inlay on an Eastern Zhou Hu Vase

Turquoise was one of the more popular inlays, but unfortunately it will degrade to dust in a number of soil conditions. It will also change colour in sunlight over time, a fact known to most Victorian jewellery collectors. The turquoise inlay (Fig. 63) on the Warring States period sword guard (Fig.194), is I think, genuinely of the period. These flat carved inlays are more likely to be faked than the cabochons, which also appeared in Warring States period swords.

Fig. 63 Turquoise Inlay in a Warring States Sword Guard

The gold and silver inlay on the 95mm long belt hook (Fig. 64, upper left) would appear to be original, as it disappears under the remains of the fabric which has embedded in the corrosion on the right hand end. The upper right gold inlaid bronze piece was probably once part of an elaborate horse bridle cheek plate or bit.

Fig. 64 Gold & Silver Inlay of the Warring States Period

CHAPTER 13

A CATALOGUE OF AFFORDABLE BRONZES

I have titled this chapter "A Catalogue of Affordable Bronzes", because they are currently available to collectors of more modest means. Most of these bronzes are available today for between say $US300 and $US15,000, some smaller pieces, being considerably less. Please note that I have not padded this book with auction catalogue-like descriptions of each piece illustrated. The illustrations clearly show the decoration, and any reader interested in say the origins of the design, can find a wealth of books on the subject.

13.1 Dings

The ding was a cooking vessel that dates from the Shang to the Han dynasties. Many were used for cooking, so there will often be soot and grease or even food remains visible.

Description: Ding
Size: 278mm H
Period: Late Shang/Early Western Zhou
(Circa 10/11th C BC)

Fig. 65 Late Shang/Early Western Zhou Studded Bronze Ding

73

The beautifully decorated ding (Fig. 65), will by its studs generally date it to the late Shang dynasty, but the design also overlapped the dynasties, so a dating of circa 3,000 years old is possibly more accurate. Note the longer studs on the gui illustrated Fig. 102.

The overhead view (Fig. 66) shows an oft-recurring feature of many of these round dings; their out of round shape.

Fig. 66 Overhead View

While I have suggested a Western Zhou dating, the ding (Fig. 67) may even be late Shang. It is one of the most frequently found types of bronze vessel, and comes in a huge variety of shapes.

Fig. 67 Western Zhou Ding

Description:	Tripod Ding
Size:	205mm H
Period:	Probably Western Zhou (1122 – 771BC)

Note the clearly visible triangular mould marks on the soot-blackened underside, and the misshapen, out of round body, when viewed from above.

Fig. 68 The Underside

Fig. 69 Overhead View

Whereas the dings of Fig.65 and Fig. 67 have solid legs, that of Fig. 70 has been cast around a clay core. This technique gave a more bulky leg, while conserving the amount and weight of the valuable bronze material used. The design on this ding suggests a Western Zhou dating, but the more "chunky" legs are usually later.

Description: Tripod Ding
Size: 240mm D
Period: Western Zhou
(1122 – 771BC)

Fig. 70 Western Zhou Ding   **Fig. 71 The Underside**

Note the mixture of patinas on this piece. Azurite blue on the inside, with cuprite red and malachite green on the exterior. The underside (Fig.71) again shows the sectional mould lines from casting.

Description: Ding
Size: 190mm D
Period: Late Western Zhou
(1122 to 771BC)

Fig. 72 Late Western Zhou Ding

The heavily cast ding (Fig. 72) and the graduated set of three (Fig. 74) show the combination of the two eras; the heavy casting of Western Zhou with the "chunky" clay cored legs of Eastern Zhou. According to the protocols of the Western Zhou, a common officer was entitled to three ding.

Note the sprue mark from casting, visible on the underside of one of the legs on this ding. (Fig.73) The clay core (arrowed) is also visible.

Fig. 73 Sprue Marks on Leg

Description: Three Graduated Ding
Size: 155, 165 & 177mm D
Period: Probably Early Eastern Zhou (770 to 256BC)

Fig. 74 Graduated Set of Three Bronze Ding

The undersides of these ding (Fig. 75) show clearly the mixture of cuprite (red) and malachite (green) corrosion, so common to many of these bronzes. These three ding appear to have been in contact with timber, perhaps upturned on a shelf, as the remains of it are embedded in the corrosion (Fig. 76).

Fig. 75 View of Undersides, Showing Mixture of Corrosion

Periodically one encounters a bronze which appears to be a mixture of two different shapes, and the ding of Fig. 77 is such an example. It is basically a bowl (gui) with legs, the design suggesting an Eastern Zhou dating. Some would call this a cauldron.

Fig. 76 Traces of Timber

Description: Ding
Size: 180mm D
Period: Eastern Zhou (770 to 256BC)

Fig.77 Eastern Zhou Ding

Description: Tripod Ding
Size: 340mm D
Period: Eastern Zhou
(770 – 256BC)

Fig. 78 Eastern Zhou Ding

The clay sectional moulds for these early bronzes seem only to have been used once, giving an enormous range of designs and shapes, as these three similar dings illustrate (Fig. 78, 79 and 82).

Description: Tripod Ding
Size: 290mm D
Period: Eastern Zhou
(770 – 256BC)

Fig. 79 Eastern Zhou Ding

Some of these designs were particularly detailed, as is illustrated by the dragon design (Fig. 80), which covers not only the lid, but also the sides of this ding. The base has been damaged and extensively repaired, as was shown earlier in the x-ray (Fig.11). The detached leg shows a body cast only 2 mm thick, an amazing technical feat given the fact it was made over 2400 years ago.

Fig. 80 Close-up of Design

Fig. 81 Underside

Description: Tripod Ding
Size: 180mm D
Period: Eastern Zhou (770 - 256BC)

Fig. 82 Eastern Zhou Ding

Fig. 83 Details of Lid Design

Fig. 84 Azurite & Malachite Corrosion on Inside of Lid

The extreme combinations of azurite (blue) and malachite (green) corrosion, as seen in the inside of the lid of this ding (Fig. 84) are something I have not seen duplicated on the fakes to date. This incidentally, is the ground colour for this book's cover.

By the Han dynasty, which commenced in 206BC, designs generally were much plainer than in the earlier periods. Bronze was obviously more plentiful, possibly because iron had replaced many of its uses, and much of the bronze was used for more functional purposes; such as cooking vessels. The small ding (Fig. 85) appears to have been made for one person, and is one of the most common shapes found in burials of this period.

Description: Tripod Ding
Size: 125mm D
Period: Han Dynasty
           (206BC – 220AD)

Fig. 85 Han Dynasty Ding
The dark patch on the lid is a repair (arrowed).

Description: Pair Of Tripod Ding
Size: 180mm D
Period: Han Dynasty (206BC to 220AD)

Fig. 86 Pair of Polished Ding

The two ding (Fig. 86) give an idea of what the original pieces must have looked like. It is quite rare to find these bronzes retaining much of their original polish. These thinly cast bronzes have a commonly encountered defect; the visible appearance of spacers (chaplets) on both surfaces, as may be seen on the outside and inside of the lids (Fig. 87 and 88).

Fig. 87 Exterior of Lid Showing Spacers

Fig. 88 Interior of Lid Showing Spacers

The ding came in a large variety of shapes and sizes, and there will be some argument that the next two illustrated pieces are in fact dings. The globe-shaped ding (or dui) (Fig. 89) is rarely seen outside Chinese museum collections, while the bowl-lidded ding (Fig. 91) is referred to as a you by the National Museum of History, and as a hu by the Asian Art Museum of San Francisco.

The dui, which retains traces of its original gilding, has been preserved in a wet environment, where the soil minerals have stopped corrosion. It was ingeniously made to open into two separate ding, the handles on the top, doubling as legs when inverted. A detached spacer (arrowed) has caused a hole in the bowl (arrowed).

Description: Globe-shaped Ding (Dui)
Size: 220mm H x 195mm Diam.
Period: Warring States (475 to 221BC)

Fig. 89 Globe-shaped Ding (or Dui)

Fig. 90 Dui (Another View)

Description: Bowl-lidded Ding (You)
Size: 180mm H
Period: Warring States (475 to 221BC)

Fig. 91 Bowl-lidded Ding (You) with Chain Handle

The elaborate swivel chain on this ding, which is remarkably similar to today's fishing swivel, seems to have first appeared in the Warring States period. The plain undecorated sides to this vessel suggests a Han dynasty date of manufacture, so my Warring States dating, may subsequently prove to require correction.

Fig. 92 Bowl-lidded Ding (You) with Chain Handle (Another View)

13.2 Dou

The dou is a pedestal based bowl, which more often than not had a lid. The only example I possess to illustrate in this chapter (Fig. 93), appears to be another of those odd combinations; a ding on a pedestal base. These very crudely cast bronzes with a high lead content (indicated by their weight) were relatively common in the early Eastern Zhou dynasty, but the absence of any decoration again suggests a later dating, possibly Western Han dynasty.

Description: Pedestal Dou
Size: 175mm H
**Period: Possibly Western Han Dynasty
            (206BC to 9AD)**

Fig. 93 Dou

13.3 Fanghu

While the fanghu is commonly referred to as a vase, its original use was as a wine vessel. The earliest fanghu that has passed through my hands is the very crudely cast example (E on the cover), which is in the vicinity of 2,500 to 2,600 years old, dating it to the Spring and Autumn period of the Eastern Zhou dynasty. These poorly cast vessels are generally believed to have been made purely for burial purposes, perhaps for someone of lesser means (Fig. 94).

Description: Lidded Fanghu
Size: 310mm H
Period: Spring & Autumn
(770 – 476BC)

Fig. 94 Spring & Autumn Fanghu

Fig. 95 Underside of Spring & Autumn Fanghu

The underside (Fig. 95) of this fanghu, once again shows the azurite blue patina, so common with many of the bases and interiors of these ancient bronze vessels.

The lidded fanghu (Fig. 96 and C on the cover), while dating later to the Warring States period, is much thinner and better finished than its older counterpart. The bare circular area around the ring handle, was probably caused by a solvent removing a repatinated area of corrosion, following a recent repair.

Description: Lidded Fanghu
Size: 420mm H
Period: Warring States
(475 to 221BC)

Fig. 96 Warring States Lidded Fanghu

13.4 Gu

The gu was a wine cup, which is usually to be found with a flaring mouth which is much wider than the base (Fig. 97). They have traditionally commanded very high prices at auction, and as a consequence, have been much copied. As I have earlier stated, a large number of these gu will be found with either a vertical hole or a cross-shaped split in the lower middle section, suggesting that there were brackets used to hold the walls apart or in place, during the casting process. Such a slit is to be seen in these examples.

Description: Gu
Size: 210mm H
Period: Western Zhou
(1122 to 771BC)

Fig. 97 Western Zhou Gu

Fig. 98 The Underside

Just out of curiosity, I had the throat of this gu x-rayed (Fig. 99). While there was no evidence of spacers, the unmistakable air bubbles from ancient casting are clearly to be seen.

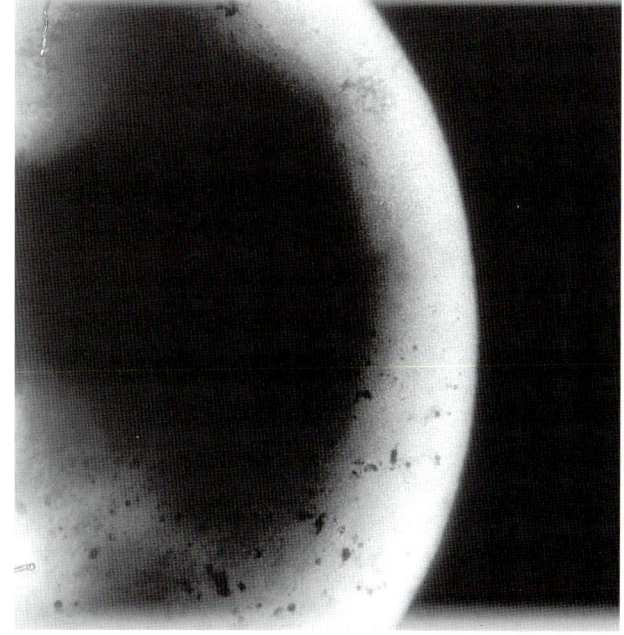

Fig. 99 X-ray of Gu Mouth

Description: Gu
Size: 260mm H
Period: Western Zhou Dynasty (1122 to 771BC)

Fig. 100 Western Zhou Gu

The close-up (Fig. 101) shows the deeply cast leiwen design, and the cross-shaped hole which probably held the bracket which kept the two moulds in place.

Fig. 101 Close-up of Leiwen Design

13.5 Gui

The gui was a relatively common food vessel, and like the ding, came in an enormous range of shapes and designs. The simplest gui was just a plain bowl, but the more elaborate ones not only had quite detailed designs, but raised feet and lids. The distinction between a gui and a pan is not always apparent, and I have no doubts that not everyone will agree to the classification as I have them.

The finest example I have had pass through my hands, is the heavily studded and decorated bowl (Fig. 102), whose design dates to the Shang dynasty, over 3,000 years ago. However, this design had a resurgence of popularity in the late Eastern Zhou so that the TL tested date of the core at 2100 years may be more accurate.

Description: Studded Gui
Size: 247mm D
Period: Late Eastern Zhou?

Fig. 102 Late Eastern Zhou? Studded Gui

Fig. 103 Underside view of Studded Gui

This gui shows the pottery core (Fig.103) which is occasionally to be found on these pieces, and to date has been a positive indicator of authenticity. I decided to x-ray this rare gu, and the x-ray of the base (Fig. 104) shows the expected air bubbles, and four strange black holes, which may have been sprue marks or ancient repairs.

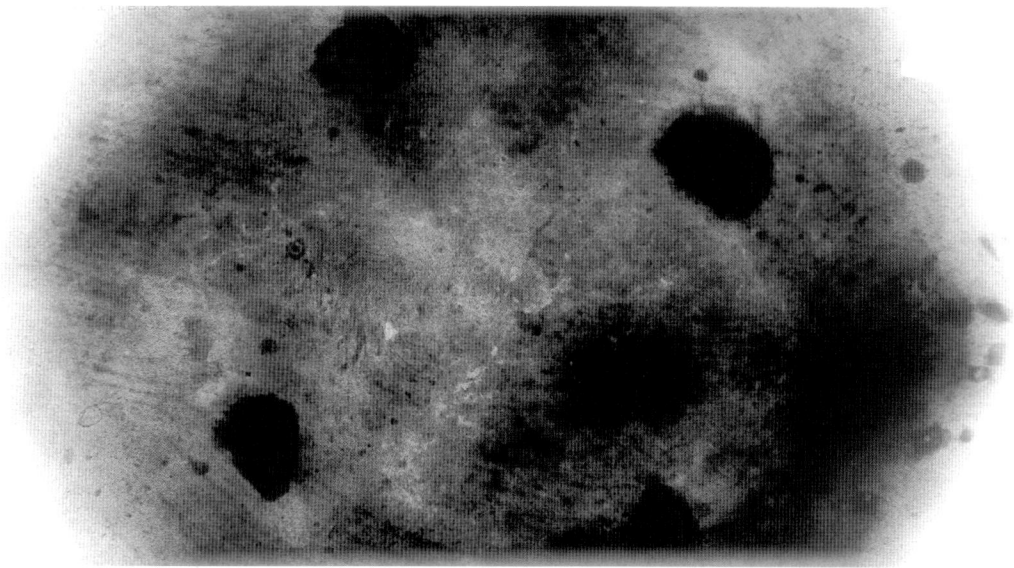

Fig. 104 X-ray of Base of Studded Gui

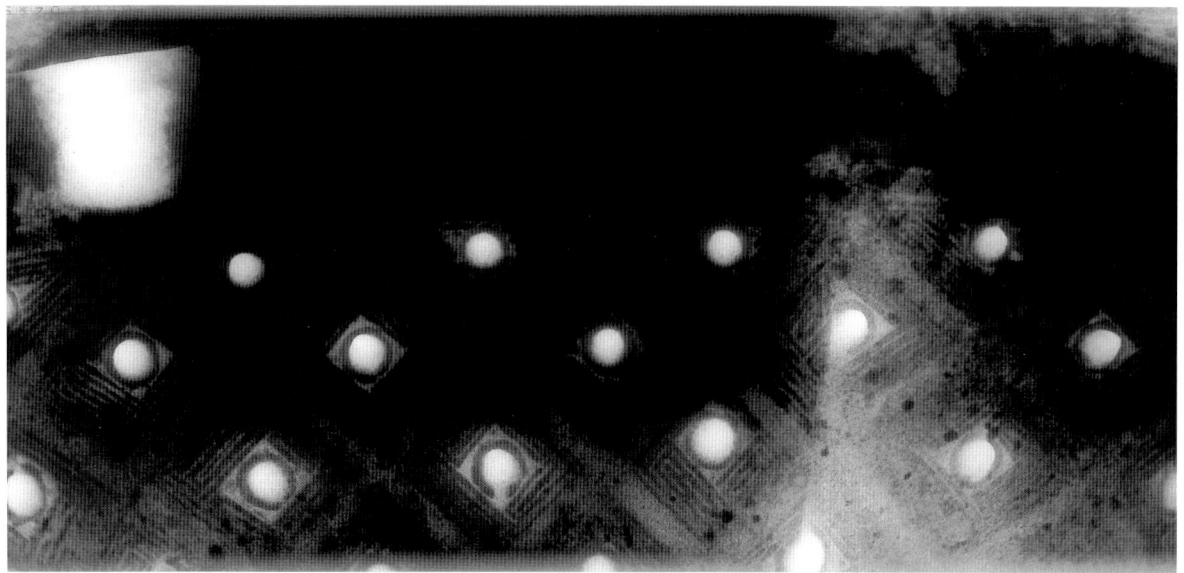

Fig. 105 X-ray of Side of Studded Gui

The x-ray of the side of this gui (Fig. 105) showed the expected air bubbles, and also another feature of the ancient casting technique, the variation in the thickness of the castings; as indicated by the darker (thinner) and lighter (thicker) sections.

The example (Fig. 106), dating to the late Western Zhou, has dragon head handles and paw feet. Shown from two angles (Fig. 107), the gui can be seen to be unevenly balanced, a relatively common flaw arising from the old casting techniques, and a defect which I have not seen to date on modern day fakes.

The underside (Fig. 108) has a clearly visible jagged line, indicating that the mould cracked during casting. Note again the inward bending rim on the base.

Description: Lidded Gui
Size: 230mm H
Period: Late Western Zhou (1122 – 771BC)

Fig. 106 Late Western Zhou Gui

Fig. 107 Another View

Fig. 108 Underside of Late Western Zhou Gui

Many of these plain more utilitarian bowls do not feature in any of the English language texts published to date, and pending further research their dating may be open to question. The round gui (Fig. 109) is such a piece, possibly dating to as early as the Spring and Autumn period, or as late as the Western Han dynasty. Fresh from a plundered grave, this one has not even had the clay deposits from burial removed.

Description: Gui
Size: 225 D
Period: Possibly Western Han Dynasty (206BC – 9AD)

Fig. 109 Plain Western Han Gui

A similar dating problem exists with the plain lidded gui (Fig.110), which in my opinion probably also dates to the Western Han dynasty. The Chinese dealer who supplied these pieces simply refers to them as Han dynasty (206BC – 220AD), giving himself a 400 year margin of error. During the late Warring States period and Han dynasty, there appear to have been some improvements to the traditional designs, and this lid has three little lugs attached, enabling it to fix exactly to the base (Fig. 111).

Description: Lidded Gui
Size: 185mm D
Period: Probably Western Han Dynasty (206BC – 9AD)

Fig. 110 Plain Western Han Lidded Gui

Note the unappealing cerussite corrosion, particularly on the lid, a common recurring feature of many Han dynasty bronzes.

Fig. 111 The Underside

13.6 He

The he was a wine cup, of (in this example) relatively large, shallow and oval shape, adorned with two ring handles on the sides. I am told that the one illustrated (Fig.112), was found with the wine jug (Fig.147), which if correct, dates it to the Spring and Autumn period, circa 2,500 plus years ago. Once again, it is seen with the typical glutinous clay adhesions, so common to many of these burial artefacts, and the bane of many collectors' lives; for the peasant farmers persist in scratching it off, in so doing, leaving scratches on the underlying bronze.

Description: He
Size: 145mm L
Period: Possibly Spring & Autumn (770 – 476BC)

Fig. 112 Spring & Autumn He

13.7 Hu

The hu is commonly referred to as a vase, but its original use was as a wine vessel. The hu came in a number of shapes, all with a bulbous body with a narrower opening at the top, some with a lid and some without. The quality of these vessels varied enormously, from the beautifully inlaid example (Fig. 113), to the plainer, more utilitarian vessels illustrated later.

Description: Inlaid Hu
Size: 300mm H
Period: Warring States (475 to 221BC)

Fig. 113 Inlaid Hu

Description: Inlaid Hu
Size: 180mm H
Period: Warring States (475 to 221BC)

Fig. 114 Inlaid Hu

Whereas the first of these hu has remnants of copper wire inlay remaining (Fig.62), there is no sign of the original inlay in the second (Fig. 115), suggesting that it may have been lacquer.

Fig. 115 Inlaid Design on Fig. 114

Some of these ancient bronze hu (Fig.116 and 117) have metal bands encircling them. Whether these were for reinforcing the piece during casting, or for decoration, I have yet to determine.

Description: Banded Hu
Size: 340mm
Period: Probably Western Han Dynasty (206BC to 9AD)

Fig. 116 Banded Hu

Description: Banded Hu
Size: 520mm H.
Period: Probably Western Han Dynasty (206BC to 9AD)

Fig. 117 Banded Hu

The banded hu (Fig. 117) is a massive 520mm (20.8 inches) tall. It has the inward bending foot rim (Fig. 118) and cuprite and malachite corrosion, which I have referred to earlier on other examples from this period.

Fig. 118 Underside View

Another variation of this shape is to be seen in the hu (Fig. 119), whose plain design and lion mask (taotie) ring handles, suggest a date of manufacture no earlier than Warring States, and more probably Han dynasty.

Description: Ring Handled Hu
Size: 325mm H.
Period: Han dynasty
(206BC to 220AD)

Fig. 119 Ring Handled Hu   **Fig. 120 Underside View**

The magnificent pair of hu vases (Fig.121) have been preserved in wet soil, and date to the same period in the Warring States as the globe-shaped ding or dui (Fig. 89), which apparently came from the same tomb.

Fig. 121 Pair of Warring States Hu

Description: Pair Of Hu
Size: 360mm H
Period: Warring States (475 to 221BC)

Fig. 122 Underside View Showing Pottery Cores

The underside view (Fig. 122) shows the inward bending rim and pottery core, found on many of the bronze vessels of this period. The close-up (Fig.123) shows an ancient repair, probably to fix a hole left by a detached spacer, one of which can be seen below and to the left of the repair.

The taotie lion mask ring handle (Fig. 124) probably came from a hu or fanghu wine jar of the Warring States/Han period. Note the ancient repair to the ring (arrowed), one of the strongest indicators that the bronze is genuinely old.

Fig. 123 Close-up of Repair & Spacer

Fig. 124 Taotie Lion Mask Ring Handle

I was wandering through the repair area in a Chinese warehouse one day in June 2001, and I spotted a bowl of taotie ring handles from broken hu and fanghu wine jars (Fig.125).

Description: Taotie Ring Handles
Size: 42 to 78mm W
Period: Warring States/W. Han Dynasty (475BC to 9AD)

Fig. 125 Taotie Ring Handles

Another variation of the hu vase, originating in the Warring States period, was that known as "garlic head" (Fig. 126), the name given obviously by the shape of the top.

Description: Two Garlic Head Hu
Size: 350 & 380mm
Period: Probably Warring States
(475 to 221BC)

Fig. 126 Garlic Head Hu

Fig. 127 Underside View

Readers will note the two totally different patinas on these two hu, undoubtedly occurring because of differing conditions of burial.

The hu (Fig. 128 and D on the cover) has the added embellishment of a drainage loop (arrowed), enabling it to be hung upside-down to dry, perhaps suggesting a later date of manufacture than the preceding two.

Description: Garlic Head Hu
Size: 37mm H
Period: Warring States (475 to 221BC)

Fig. 128 "Garlic Head" Hu   **Fig. 129 Underside View**

We see again the inward bending foot rim and the blue azurite patina (Fig. 129), so common to the undersides of many of these excavated ancient bronzes.

The small garlic head hu (Fig. 130) is, in my experience, quite rare. Standing just 190mm high, and probably made for one person, it must have held approximately half the contents of the larger more common examples.

Description: Small Hu
Size: 190mm H
Period: Warring States
(475 to 221BC)

Fig. 130 Small Garlic Head Hu   **Fig. 131 Underside View**

The strange "flattened" garlic head hu (Fig. 132 and 133) is much less common than the round examples, and must date to the late Warring States period or Western Han dynasties.

Description: Flattened Garlic Head Hu
Size: 250mm H
Period: Warring States/Western Han
(475BC to 9AD)

Fig. 132 "Flattened" Garlic Head Hu

Fig. 133 Angled View of Flattened Garlic Hu

13.8 Jia

The jia (sometimes referred to as chia or chueh) was a tripod vessel used for heating wine. It is often found in conjunction with the jue, and usually dates to the Shang or Western Zhou dynasties. The example (Fig. 134) is possibly as late as Western Zhou, circa 10th century BC. For x-rays of this rare jia, please see Fig. 244 to 246.

Description: Jia
Size: 240mm H
Period: Shang Dynasty
(1766 to 1122BC)

Fig. 134 Jia

Fig. 135 Underside View

13.9 Li

The li was a tripod cooking vessel not dissimilar to the ding, its primary difference being that its three legs were formed like goat teats (Fig. 136).

Description: Li
Size: 230mm H
Period: Probably Western Zhou (1122 to 771BC)

Fig. 136 Li

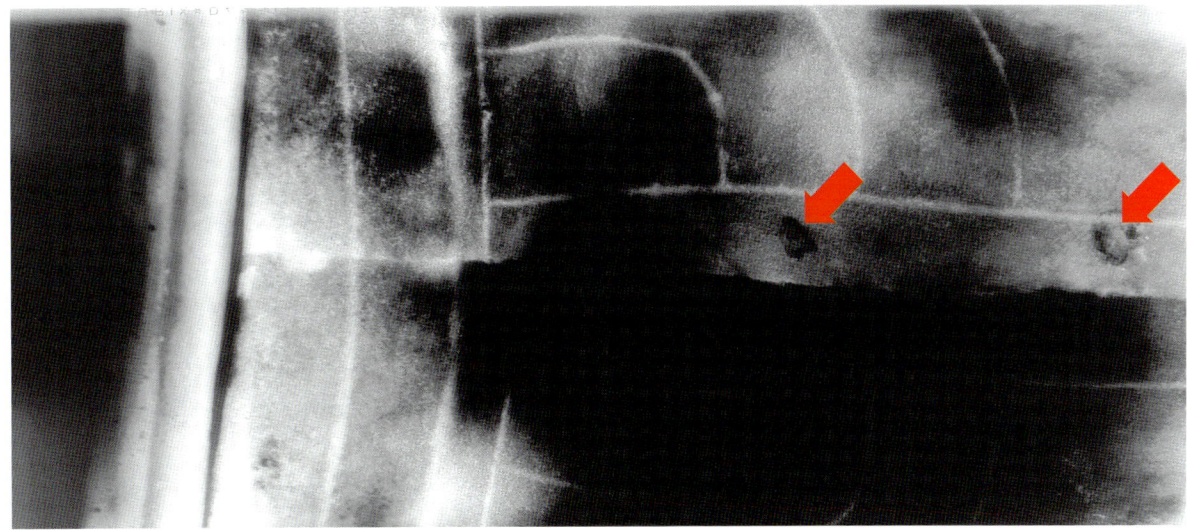

Fig. 137 X-ray of Li Showing Spacers

Many of these li date to the Shang dynasty, over 3,000 years ago, but the very thin walls of this example, suggest a later dating.

13.9 Pan

The pan was a domestic bowl used for washing. Most of these particularly thin pieces, such as the twin fish bowl (Fig. 138), must be of later date, possibly Warring States period, Qin or Han dynasty. It is interesting to note the twin fish design, which is often associated with marriage in Chinese lore, appearing at such an early date. The distinction between a pan, a gui, a jian, and a yu is not always apparent, as in this example.

Description: Pan
Size: 340mm D
Period: Probably Late Warring States (475 to 221BC)

Fig. 138 Pan Decorated with Twin Fish

Fig. 139 Underside View   **Fig. 140 Twin Fish Design**

Note again the mould casting lines (Fig. 139) and the uneven distribution of the metal in the x-ray (Fig. 141).

Fig. 141 X-ray of Twin Fish Pan

13.10 Xian (or Yan)

The xian or yan was a steamer, with a grilled upper pot over a lower pot which contained water. It came in either two sections (Fig.142), or three sections (Fig. 144).

Description: Xian (or Yan)
Size: 475H x 337D
Period: Warring States
(475 to 221BC)

Fig. 142 Warring States Xian

Fig. 143 Underside View

Description: Xian
Size: 370mm H
Period: Han Dynasty (206BC to 220AD)

Fig. 144 Massive Han Dynasty Xian

Fig 145 Three Sectional View

The elaborate metal grilles (Fig. 146) are a feature of not only these xian, but also the stoves illustrated later. Note also the rust stains, from burial contact with an iron object.

Fig. 146 Close-up of Steamer Grille

13.11 Yi

The yi was a wine jug, probably used in ritual toasting to the ancestors. The example illustrated (Fig. 147) has a very plainly decorated head, presumably intended to represent a dragon.

Description: Yi
Size: 240mm L
Period: Spring & Autumn
(770 to 476BC)

Fig. 147 Yi

Fig. 148 Underside View

13.12 Other Vessels

I have also illustrated a number of ancient bronze pieces, for which the Chinese name is either not appropriate, or not in common use. These include a complete tomb garniture, incense burners, lamps and stoves.

Description: Tomb Garniture
Size: Fanghu are 163mm H
Period: Spring & Autumn (770 to 476BC)

Fig. 149 Ten Piece Tomb Garniture

The rare tomb garniture (Fig.149) comprises ten pieces; a graduated set of three ding, two fanghu, two lidded gui, one unlidded gui, and two axle caps and cotter pins. These all came from a single tomb that dated to the Spring and Autumn period, circa 2,500 years ago.

The close-up of the axle caps and cotter pin, (Fig. 150) shows a cat's head, almost Egyptian in appearance. These axle caps are generally believed to have come from chariots, which along with the horses, were buried in the tombs to accompany the deceased in the afterlife.

The practise of these wasteful burials was supposedly outlawed in the Qin dynasty (circa 220BC), the slaves, concubines, horses, dogs etc being replaced thereafter by pottery and wood replicas.

Fig. 150 Close-up of Axle Cap

Description: Censer?
Size: 135 mm D
Period: Possibly Warring States (475 to 221BC)

Fig. 151 Censer?

Fig. 152 View of Lid

The intricately decorated vessel (Fig. 151), which must once have had a long wood handle, was obviously designed like a ding to sit on a fire. The holed lid (Fig. 152) suggests that it may have been used for burning incense, but I am by no means certain of that. Dating is also a matter of some debate, and the elaborate decoration, in my opinion, suggests a pre-Han date of manufacture.

The hill censer (Fig. 153) is sometimes called bo shan lu, and is one of the more common shapes of the Han dynasty, coming in a variety of sizes. This one has dragon decoration around the base.

Description: **Hill Censer**
Size: **120mm**
Period: **Han dynasty**
(206BC to 220AD)

Fig. 153 Hill Censer

Fig. 154 Underside View

Description: Censer
Size: 160mm D
Period: Han dynasty (206BC to 220AD)

Fig. 155 Censer

The incense burner or censer (Fig.155) probably dates to the Western Han dynasty, over 2,000 years ago. This pedestal type censer also comes in a variety of shapes and sizes, ranging from this relatively small plain example, with a bird finial, to larger ones with intricately cast and moulded base and top.

Description: Double Lamp
Size: 100mm D
Period: Probably Spring & Autumn (770 to 476BC)

Fig. 156 Double Lamp

The lamp (Fig.156) is a very unusual piece, the like of which I have not seen previously. Dating probably to the Spring and Autumn period, it opens up to reveal two lamps. Look carefully at the front of this lamp, and the remains of ancient fabric (arrowed) in the corrosion can be seen. The azurite corrosion inside the lid, suggests that the fabric must have covered the lid, which also suggests that it was buried in the closed position.

Fig. 157 The Two Lamps Revealed

Description: Lamp
Size: 63mm H
Period: Han dynasty (206BC to 220AD)

Fig. 158 Lamp

The little bronze lamp (Fig. 158) is one of the most common items to be found in tombs of the Han period. Obviously intended for one person, they appear to have survived in relatively large numbers. Also surviving in relatively large numbers, are the ancient bronze stoves (tzau) (Fig. 159), designed for one person, usually made with two egg poachers and a steamer. The second stove from the right, has a bowl in place of the steamer. Note the dragon head chimney on each one. When I first saw these, I assumed that they must have been filled with water inside the hollow section, but if this was the case, then every one has lost the back cover. Perhaps they were filled with grass or twigs and placed over a fire? I have yet to clarify this point.

Description: Four Stoves (Tzau)
Size: 165mm to 220mm L
Period: Han dynasty (206BC to 220AD)

Fig. 159 Four Stoves (Tzau)

13.13 Coins

Coins must have been the most commonly cast items made in the history of Chinese bronze casting, and have been the subject of a number of specialist books on the subject. I illustrate (Fig 160) examples of the more common coins made in the Han dynasty or earlier. The uppermost two are spade coins dating to the Warring States period. With a fired clay core, they should be dateable by thermoluminescence testing, although my one attempt at doing so provided an unreliable dating of 280 years old. The five central coins are all from the Han dynasty, while the lower knife shaped coin was declared to be a fake, by the American Numismatic Society, a fact disputed by another experienced European coin dealer.

Fig. 160 Ancient Chinese Bronze Coins

I cannot possibly do justice to the subject of Chinese coins within the confines of this book, and refer readers to the books, in the bibliography, some of which, because their titles are in Chinese, are variously translated.

13.14 Mirrors

Mirrors made of bronze, the face originally highly polished and the back usually decorated, though sometimes plain, were a popular item in the Han dynasty.

They were of course made prior to this period, but such pieces are nowhere near as common. Of all the various Chinese bronze pieces, mirrors are arguably the most difficult to date with certainty; particularly if they have been cleaned. The mirrors (Fig. 161) are all of Han dynasty style, but the bottom mirror is undoubtedly a fake. In an endeavour to see if it would assist with authentication, I had these four mirrors x-rayed. As can be seen from the x-ray (Fig. 162), the only sign of any air bubbles, which are to be found in many of the ancient cast vessels, is in the largest mirror.

Description: Four Mirrors
Size: 60 to 100mm D
Period: Han Dynasty (3) & Fake (206BC to 220AD)

Fig. 161 Four Mirrors Of Han Style

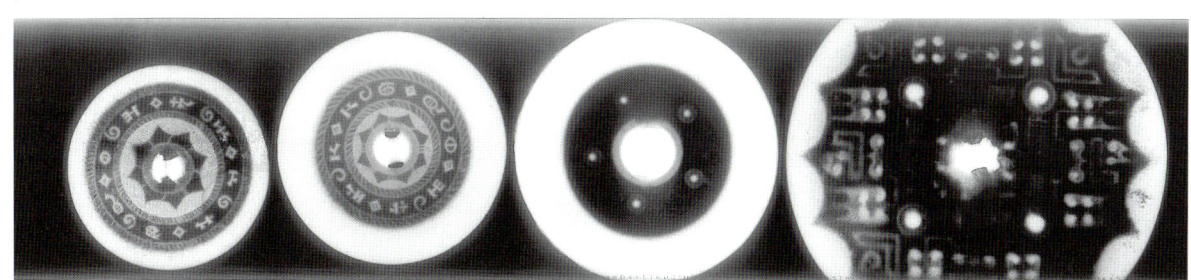

Fig. 162 X-Ray of Four Mirrors

In a further endeavour to see if another group of mirrors showed any features which might assist in authentication, I x-rayed another different fake and genuine Han mirror. In this instance, the smaller fake showed what appeared to be air bubbles, while the larger genuine Han mirror revealed a crack concealed under the corrosion. My admittedly restricted x-ray testing of mirrors did not reveal any feature which was helpful in dating, and now, because of the high quality fakes available, I do not buy mirrors, other than from my regular sources, unless I can visually see some external confirmation of age; such as fabric in the corrosion. (Fig. 164 to 167).

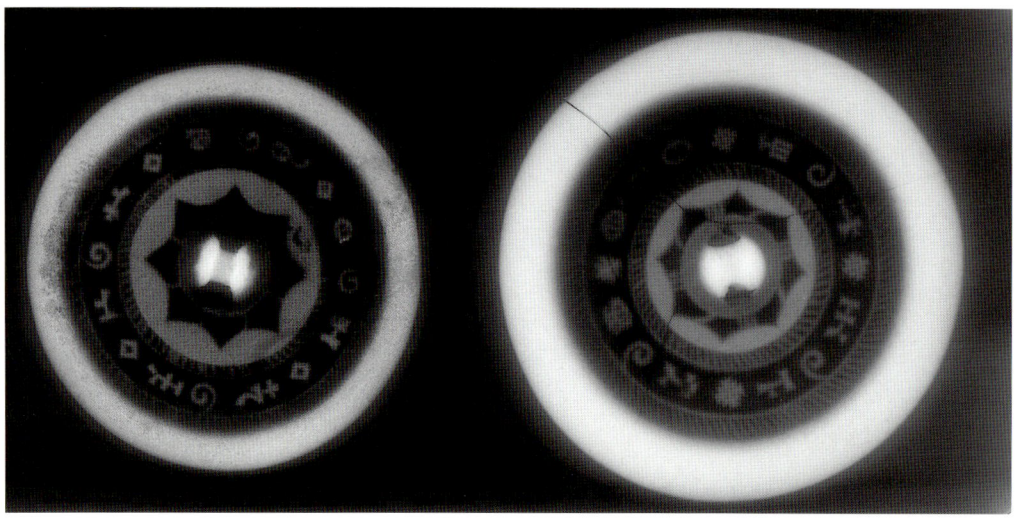

Fig. 163 X-Ray of Two Han Style Mirrors

Description: Two Mirrors
Size: 105 & 103mm D
Period: Han Dynasty (206BC to 220AD)

Fig. 164 Two Han Dynasty Mirrors

Fig. 165 The Reverse View

Description: Six Mirrors
Size: 90 to 115mm D
Period: Han Dynasty (206BC to 220AD)

Fig. 166 Six Han Dynasty Mirrors

Fig. 167 The Reverse View

Like coins, ancient Chinese bronze mirrors are a specialist field, and there are a number of books on the subject. I refer readers to:

Decorated Historic Bronze Mirrors By North River Publishing Co
ISBN 7-5310-0721-5/J.646

13.15 Miscellaneous Bronze Artefacts

There were numerous articles of bronze made for daily use, and many of these are seldom seen in the West. The items that follow were purchased by the author, solely for illustration in this book. The small bronze bells illustrated (Fig. 168) were once attached to the harness of chariot horses, as were the bridle bits. They must have been a common burial piece in the Han and Warring States periods, as I have sold several hundred of these bells over the years, and several dozen bridle bits.

Description: Bells & Bridle Bits
Size: Bells 52 to 67mm W
Bits 200 to 223 L
Period: Western Han or Warring States (475BC to 9AD)

Fig. 168 Bells & Bridle Bits

One of the most common items of personal adornment made of bronze, was the belt or garment hook. As the ones illustrated show (Fig. 169), they came in a huge range of shapes and sizes.

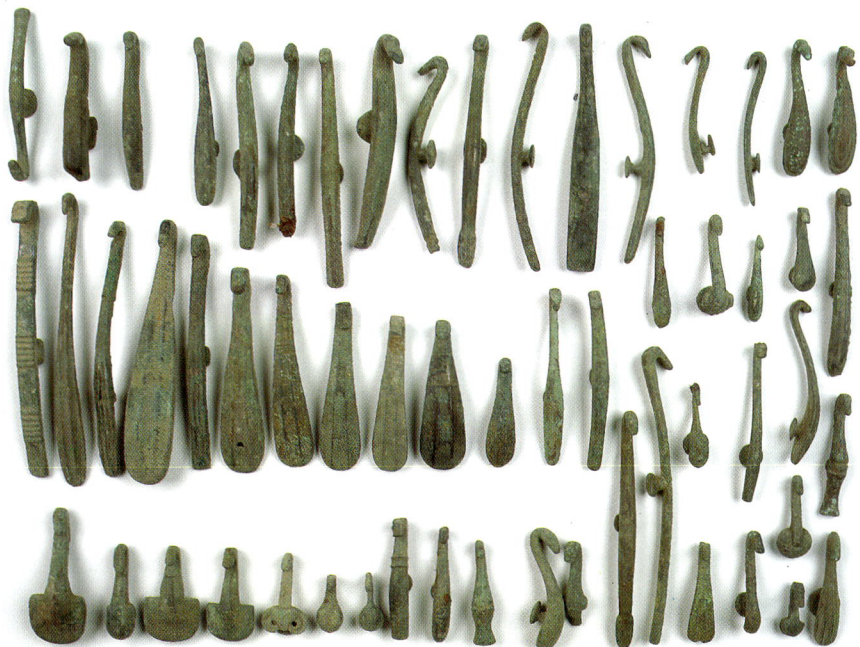

Description: 58 Belt or Garment Hooks
Size: 34mm to 170mm L
Period: Han or Warring States (475BC to 220AD)

Fig. 169 58 Different Belt or Garment Hooks

An additional three belt hooks, shown to larger scale, are illustrated (Fig. 170)

Description: Three Belt Hooks
Size: 100 to 153mm
Period: Han or Warring States
(475BC to 220AD)

Fig. 170 Three Belt Hooks

Chinese costume of this period, in addition to using belt and garment hooks, also occasionally used bronze buttons (Fig. 171).

Fig. 171 Two Buttons

Chariot axle hub caps are found in many tombs of the Han and Warring States periods, and they were sometimes plain, sometimes profusely decorated (Fig. 172).

Description: Chariot Axle Hub
Size: 75mm L
Period: Probably Warring States
(475 to 221BC)

Fig. 172 Chariot Axle Hub & Pin

Bronze utensils were also made for domestic use, and some of them are remarkably similar to those made today. Knives, spoons and ladles, two of which I have to illustrate (Fig. 173 and 174), are sometimes found. The first would have once had a wood handle attached.

Description: Ladle or Scoop
Size: 150mm
Period: Han dynasty
(206BC to 220AD)

Fig. 173 Ladle or Scoop

Description: Ladle
Size: 273mm L
Period: Han dynasty
(206BC to 220AD).

Fig. 174 Long Handled Ladle

Occasionally, bronze items turn up, whose original use is sometimes a matter of debate. The fierce animal head (Fig.175) is a case in point, because it was sold to me as a shoulder guard off a soldier's uniform, but another dealer has suggested it was a nose protector on a chariot horse, and yet another that it was a spirit scarer from a door. Note the loops on the reverse (Fig. 176).

Description: Animal Head Ornament
Size: 97mm H x 105mm W
Period: Eastern Zhou Dynasty
(770 to 256BC)

Fig. 175 Animal Head Ornament

Fig. 176 Reverse View

13.16 Weapons

Bronze was often used in the manufacture of Chinese weapons of all descriptions. There have been a number of books written on this specialist subject, and I encourage readers to obtain copies of the following excellent texts:

Illustrated Catalogue Of Ancient Chinese Bronze Weaponry In The National Palace Museum, ISBN 957-562-199-9

Shang and Zhou Chinese Bronze Weaponry, by C.H. Wang (No ISBN)

Ancient Chinese Weapons – A Collection Of Pictures, by Cheng Dong and Zhong Shao-yi, ISBN 7-5065-0646-7/K.57

The illustrations that follow have been taken from some of the hundreds of pieces that I have sold in the past few years. They are in no particular order, and are intended only to complement the pieces shown in the above-mentioned texts.

The arrow heads (Fig. 177), of which the longest is 67mm, show a range of sizes and shapes. Sold to me as Han dynasty, some may be even earlier. The two lower right metal ends were believed, by the Chinese dealer who supplied them, to be the ends of crossbow arrows. However, my subsequent inquiries indicate that they are generally believed to be the ends of parasol canes, probably attaching to a chariot.

Fig. 177 Arrow Ends & Parasol Tips

The bronze ge, or dagger-axe, is one of the most frequently encountered of all Chinese weapons. Mounted on a wooden pole, perhaps as many as three to a pole, these pole arms must have been lethal in combat. The first two illustrated (Fig. 178) date respectively from the Shang dynasty, to the late Western Zhou. Short incised inscriptions are not uncommon during this early period, and unfortunately, as I have previously stated, many have been added at a later date.

Description: Dagger-Axe or Ge
Size: 267 & 183mm L
Period: Shang Dyn. & Late Western Zhou (Circa 3,100 & 2,800 years old)

Fig. 178 Two Dagger-axe Heads (Ge)

Description: Two Axe Heads
Size: 170 & 205mm L
Period: Shang Dynasty
(1766 to 1122BC)

Fig. 179 Two Axe Heads

The two superb axe heads (Fig. 179) date from the Shang dynasty, over 3,000 years ago. The intense red colour of one indicates a high copper content, but note the wonderful azurite and malachite patina on the other (Fig. 180). This latter axe has traces of the original timber pole attaching to the inside.

Fig. 180 Close-up of Patina

Another ge, also from the late Western Zhou dynasty (Fig. 181), shows a blistering type of corrosion which is sometimes encountered with these early bronzes. Commonly referred to as bald patches, this is generally believed to be the effect of tin oxide corrosion; which results in the thin outer crust of malachite dislodging, leaving a smooth pale green patina of tin oxide beneath (arrowed).

Description: Dagger-Axe (Ge)
Size: 184mm L
Period: Late Western Zhou (1122 to 771BC)

Fig. 181 Dagger-axe or Ge

The dating of the inscribed ge (Fig. 182) is a matter for some debate. The slightly curving blade suggests that it could be as early as the Western Zhou dynasty. The inscription was illustrated earlier (Fig. 59), and is to say the least, suspect.

Description: Dagger-Axe (Ge)
Size: 205 L. x 120 H
Period: Possibly Western Zhou
(1122 to 771BC)

Fig. 182 Dagger-axe (Ge)

Description: Three Dagger-Axes (Ge)
Size: 200 to 250mm L
Period: Possibly Warring States
(475 to 221BC)

Fig. 183 Three Dagger-Axes (Ge)

The three dagger-axes (Fig.183) are very lightly constructed, and the gilding on the top two suggests that they may have been used for ceremonial purposes, rather than warfare. The lowest ge of the three has no axe, indicating that it was the second or third ge in a multiple-mounted pole arm.

The next two ge (Fig.184) are also quite rare. The uppermost ge, with horizontal slits, probably dates to the late Western Zhou dynasty, or perhaps early Spring and Autumn. The lower ge, with an inscription, is most likely from the Warring States period, some four hundred years later.

Description: Two Dagger-Axes (Ge)
Size: 188 & 210mm L
Period: Possibly Late Western Zhou & Late Warring States

Fig. 184 Two Ge

In addition to the dagger-axe, the Chinese soldiers depended a lot on the spear, and while the wood shafts to which they were attached have usually long since rotted away, the bronze spear heads have often survived. It is not uncommon to find the remains of the timber shaft and/or binding preserved inside these spear heads.

Description: Spear Head
Size: 250mm L
Period: Shang Dynasty
(1766 to 1122BC)

Fig. 185 Spear Head

I had this spear head (G on the cover) x-rayed (Fig. 186), revealing air bubbles similar to those seen on ancient bronze vessels. Note how narrow this spear head is at the centre. Could this spear have been deliberately made to break off inside ones enemy?

133

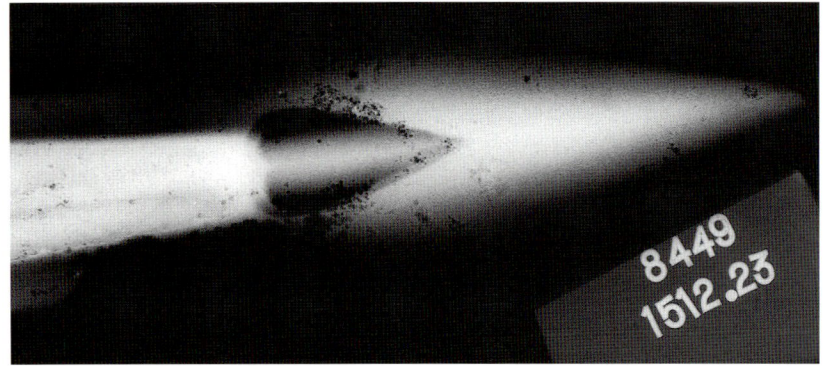

Fig. 186 X-ray of Spear Head

The range of weapon shapes made must have been immense, and it is unlikely that any collection will have every example. A minority of these weapons were decorated, as may be seen on one spear head (Fig. 187). The shape of some of these weapons, such as the axe head (with traces of fabric in the corrosion) and the knives, suggests that they probably had a domestic use as well.

Description: Five Spear Heads, A Ge & An Axe
Size: 118 to 230mm L
Period: Shang to Han Dynasties (3,000 to 2,000 Years Old)

Fig. 187 A Selection of Weapons

When I buy these cheaper weapons, the deal is usually for a quantity, and the mixture of knives, axes, ge and sword blades (Fig. 188) was one such purchase.

Description: Various Bronze Weapons
Size: Various
Period: Han Dynasty, & earlier. (Over 2,000 years)

Fig. 188 A Further Selection of Ancient Weapons

The beautifully rounded axe head (Fig. 189) dates to the Eastern Zhou dynasty, yet remains sharp after over 2,200 years of burial.

Description: Axe Head
Size: 103mm L
Period: Eastern Zhou Dynasty
(770 to 256 BC)

Fig. 189 Eastern Zhou Axe Head

In addition to these hand to hand combat weapons, the Chinese also had bows and arrows, the most fearsome of which was the crossbow. While the wood crossbows themselves have almost invariably rotted away, the bronze mechanisms (Fig. 190 and 191) have sometimes survived. Ranging in length from 117 to 125mm, these intricate mechanisms remain a testament to the Han dynasty bronze casters' skills.

Description: Crossbow Mechanism
Size: 117mm W x 140mm D
Period: Han Dynasty
(206BC to 220AD)

Fig. 190 Crossbow Mechanism　　　　**Fig. 191 Another**

With the exception perhaps of the Northern tribes, the Chinese soldier of this early period did not appear to carry knives or daggers; the surviving bladed weapons, ranging from approximately 250mm in length and up, being called short swords. The dagger (Fig.192) is a curious exception, its lightly constructed frame suggesting a non-military use. In fact, my non-English speaking supplier indicated that this was used for fishing; an explanation I can neither support nor disprove, as I cannot recall seeing another. However, I have subsequently learned of an ancient Chinese tale about an Emperor who was killed by a servant who concealed a knife inside a fish.

Description: Dagger
Size: 225mm L
Period: Possibly Han Dynasty (206BC to 220AD)

Fig. 192 Dagger

Just prior to completing this book I acquired another dagger (Fig. 193), or as the Chinese prefer to call them, short swords, and have unfortunately not had the time to research it. I suspect that it is from Northern China, and its patination suggests a Han dynasty dating. But that for the moment must be considered speculation.

Description: Dagger
Size: 290mm L
Period: Possibly Han Dynasty (206BC to 220AD)

Fig. 193 Dagger

The first bronze short swords appeared in the late Shang dynasty, but the apex of Chinese sword casting techniques was arguably in the Warring States period; when long swords, with laminated (higher tin content) blades and exquisite inlaid designs were crafted. The higher tin content enabled these swords to take a sharp edge. The example (Fig. 194) dates to the Warring States period, and the guard decoration is in turquoise. Turquoise is an unstable element, and can degrade to nothing in certain burial environments. As a consequence, much turquoise inlay is a recent enhancement.

Description: Inlaid Sword
Size: 470mm L
Period: Warring States (475 to 221BC)

Fig. 194 Inlaid Bronze Sword

Although the inlay has more often than not disappeared, the beauty of these guards can still be visualised by the unfilled design, as the uppermost sword (Fig. 195 and 196) illustrates. The lower, darker sword, is a modern fake, purchased to illustrate for comparison.

Description: Genuine & Fake Swords
Size: 523 & 480mm L
Period: Warring States & Modern

Fig. 195 Genuine & Fake Warring States Swords

Fig. 196 Close-up of Handles & Guards

Fig. 197 Close-up of Scabbard Remains

Fig. 198 Fake Green Patina

In the close-up (Fig. 197), the remains of the ancient wood and lacquer scabbard can be seen attaching to the corrosion (arrowed); a relatively common occurrence with these old swords. The patina in close-up (Fig. 198) on the fake sword, is seen to be green paint. The end of the pommel on the Warring States sword, shows a curious concentric circle design, which suggests that it may once have held an inlay. Compare this pommel, with the sharply edged fake (Fig. 21), and the difference is easily detectable.

Fig. 199 Wavering Blade on Warring States Sword

I took an angled photograph (Fig. 199), to show the distinct bend in the sword blade, possibly caused through long burial. The final check I did on these two swords, was to x-ray them (Fig.200). The old casting flaws are readily discernible in the handle of the early sword (uppermost).

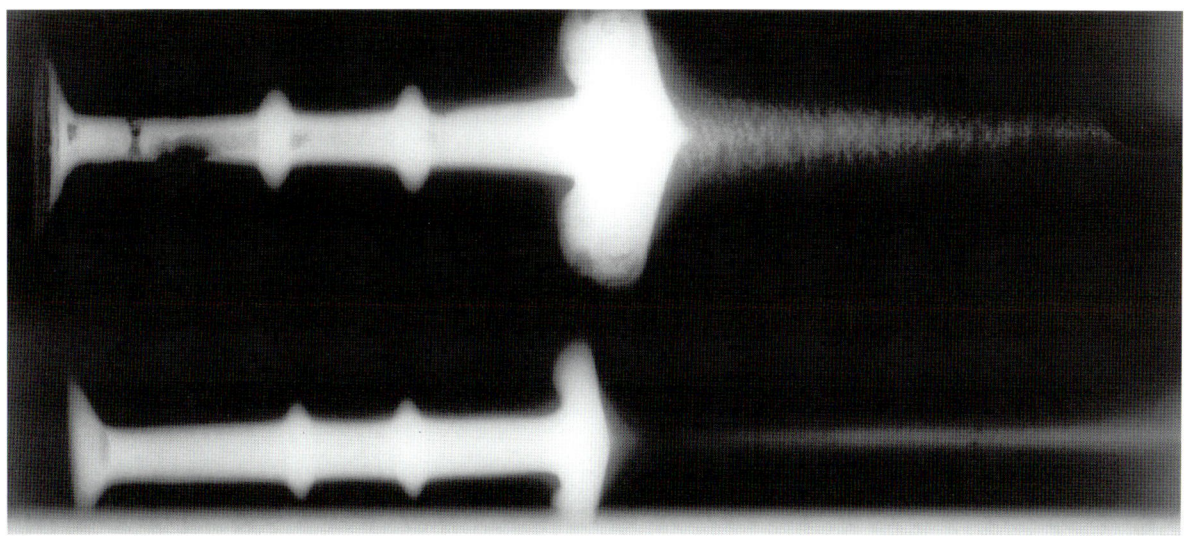

Fig. 200 X-ray of Grips on Genuine & Fake Swords

The three swords illustrated (Fig. 201) provide the reader with the opportunity again to compare two genuine swords with a modern fake.

Description: Three Swords (One Fake)
Size: 485, 463 & 510mm L
Period: Two Warring States, one modern

Fig. 201 Two Warring States & One Modern Fake Swords

The upper two swords (Fig.201) are from the Warring States, or perhaps early Western Han periods. The lower sword is a very high quality fake, whose appearance on the market when they first hit Hong Kong, caught out a number of experienced dealers, myself included. I have illustrated a close-up of the three grips and guards (Fig. 202), just to show how difficult it can be to tell the genuine from the fake.

Even closer examination shows some features which give some reassurance; notably the binding on the grip on the uppermost sword handle (Fig. 203), and the wood in the corrosion of the middle sword (Fig.204).

Fig. 202 Close-up of Three Sword Grips & Guards

Fig. 203 Binding Remains on Grip

Fig. 204 Timber Remains

The next sword (Fig. 205) is perhaps a little later, its plain design suggesting a Western Han date of manufacture.

Description: Sword
Size: 390mm
Period: Probably Western Han Dynasty (206BC to 9AD)

Fig. 205 Western Han Sword

Once again we see in the close-up (Fig. 206), the remains of the scabbard, adjacent in this case to the left side of the guard.

Fig. 206 Scabbard Remains

Chinese bronze swords of this era came in a range of shapes and sizes, including some very fine "key hole" swords, some of surprising length, as the example (Fig. 207) from the Han dynasty illustrates.

Description: Long Sword
Size: 635mm
Period: Han Dynasty (206BC to 220AD)

Fig. 207 Long "Key Hole" Sword

During the Western Han dynasty (220BC to 9AD), a lot of the sword blades became narrower, and many (Fig. 208) are found with ring handles. These ring handles are also found on the iron bladed swords of this period.

Description: Ring Handled Sword
Size: 425mm L
Period: Han Dynasty (206BC to 220AD)

Fig. 208 Ring Handled Sword

The invention of iron smelting, in the Warring States period, revolutionised the manufacture of weapons; and iron bladed swords replaced the more expensive bronze. Unfortunately, iron usually rusts to nothing when buried, and unless conditions for preservation were excellent, very few iron-bladed weapons have survived. The sword (Fig. 209), shown with two bronze handles from iron-bladed swords, is a rare exception.

Description: Iron-bladed Sword & Two Bronze Handles
Size: 430mm L
Period: Han Dynasty (206BC to 220AD)

Fig. 209 Iron bladed sword & bronze sword handles

This sword also provided the very rare opportunity to see the actual cord binding on the grips on these swords (Fig. 210).

Fig. 210 Close-up of Binding

In early 2,000 I was fortunate to be able to acquire over 50 bronze sword handles, all allegedly from one hoard, presumably buried by a retreating or defeated army. I illustrate twelve of these handles here (Fig. 211). Some of these handles are so small, that they may have been made for women or children.

Description: Twelve Sword Handles (Grips)
Size: 110 to 210mm L
Period: Probably Han Dynasty (206BC to 220AD).

Fig. 211 Twelve Han Dynasty Bronze Sword Handles

Many of the pole arms which bore the ge, also had bronze feet made for them, some with elaborate designs, some plain (Fig. 212).

Description: Pole Arm Feet
Size: 135 & 132mm L
Period: Warring States/Han Dynasties

Fig. 212 Pole Arm Feet

The undecorated pole arm foot still has the wood remaining inside, along with the original binding which kept it firmly attached to the pole (Fig. 213)

Fig. 213 Close-up of Binding

To conclude this chapter, I illustrate (Fig. 214) two pieces that again demonstrate the effects of the ravages of time. All that remains of this once impressively decorated sword, are the remains of two badly corroded bronze sword guards.

Fig. 214 Two Bronze Sword Guards

CHAPTER 14

FAKES & FORGERIES
& THEIR DETECTION

Probably the most frequently asked question from my customers, is "How do I know such and such a bronze is genuine?" I sometimes reply, as I often do with Chinese porcelain, that I liken it to being asked "How does one balance on a bicycle?" The answer, unhelpfully, is experience, for it is often the consideration of a combination of factors which enables one to make such a determination. A few that come to mind; design, shape, weight, corrosion, patination, colour, mould joins, spacers, x-rays, and one of the most important, price.

Now I have mentioned the importance of the price before, only to be roundly abused by an internet chat group which included several dishonest dealers selling a variety of fake bronzes and jades, all feeding off a small group of naïve private collectors who believed their purchases were genuine. There is a very old saying to be remembered, *"If the price is too good to be true, the item probably isn't too good"*. This especially applies to the most commonly encountered fakes; namely figures of animals, animal (or human) head ewers, jugs and other vessels, and bronze vessels which are illustrated in auction or museum catalogues. Do not expect to buy a genuine $150,000 Chinese bronze for $1,500. You may be incredibly lucky, but chances are you are being set up.

It is a good idea, if one is contemplating a major purchase from a dealer with whom one has had no prior dealings, to test the dealer's honesty by inquiring about the age of some items in his/her shop, about which there are no doubts; perhaps a 19th century Canton famille rose dish. If you are told, as I have been, ages ranging from 400 to 1,200 years old, you should immediately be on the alert.

If the purchase is a major one, get a detailed receipt, having first discussed the vendor's refund policy, should the bronze prove to be other than as stated. Then have the piece x-rayed and the pottery core (if present), thermoluminescence tested. Finally, take it to another experienced dealer, auction house, or museum, for appraisal and, if possible, valuation.

However, the secret of authentication is to look not only for what is there, but for what is not there. ie the things which the copyist has overlooked. I have for the purpose of illustrating these points, purchased in the markets of China, a number of fake bronzes.

The lidded dou (Fig. 215) has been beautifully decorated, and would fool all but the expert. Note the white patches of encrustation (salts) which are on this piece, because they are a regular occurrence on many fake bronzes, and I have yet to see them on a genuine archaic bronze.

Description: **Fake Dou**
Size: **85mm D**
Period: **Circa 2,000 AD**

Fig. 215 Modern Copy of an Eastern Zhou Dou

In fact, the trend today, as more and more fakes are produced, is to either have little if any corrosion, or masses of it, often an unappealing grey/white colour, both features readily distinguishing fakes immediately to the trained eye.

The inner view of this dou (Fig. 216) shows a cursory attempt at patination, the corrosion covered in an obviously applied coating of mud, and flaking in places.

The close-up (Fig. 217) should immediately alert the reader to a fake; or if not a fake, a re-patinated bronze. Note the obviously faked cuprite (red) corrosion, together with the appearance of corrosion, highlighting the decoration. Compare this decoration with the many close-ups of decoration on genuine ancient bronzes illustrated in this book, and the differences are apparent. ie If the decoration is highlighted by dirt or corrosion, the piece is suspect, and the person inspecting it, should be alert for other deficiencies.

Fig. 216 Inside View of Fake Dou

Another feature to note on many of these new bronzes, is the particularly dark colour of the bronze. While this colour is admittedly to be found on some genuine archaic bronzes, black is not the predominant colour.

However, the final test, if one had any further doubts about it, is to x-ray the piece. As the x-ray of the lid (Fig.218) shows, there is a complete absence of the expected spacers, no irregularities in the flow, no old repairs, and no air bubbles in the bronze.

Fig. 217 Close-up of Fake Decoration

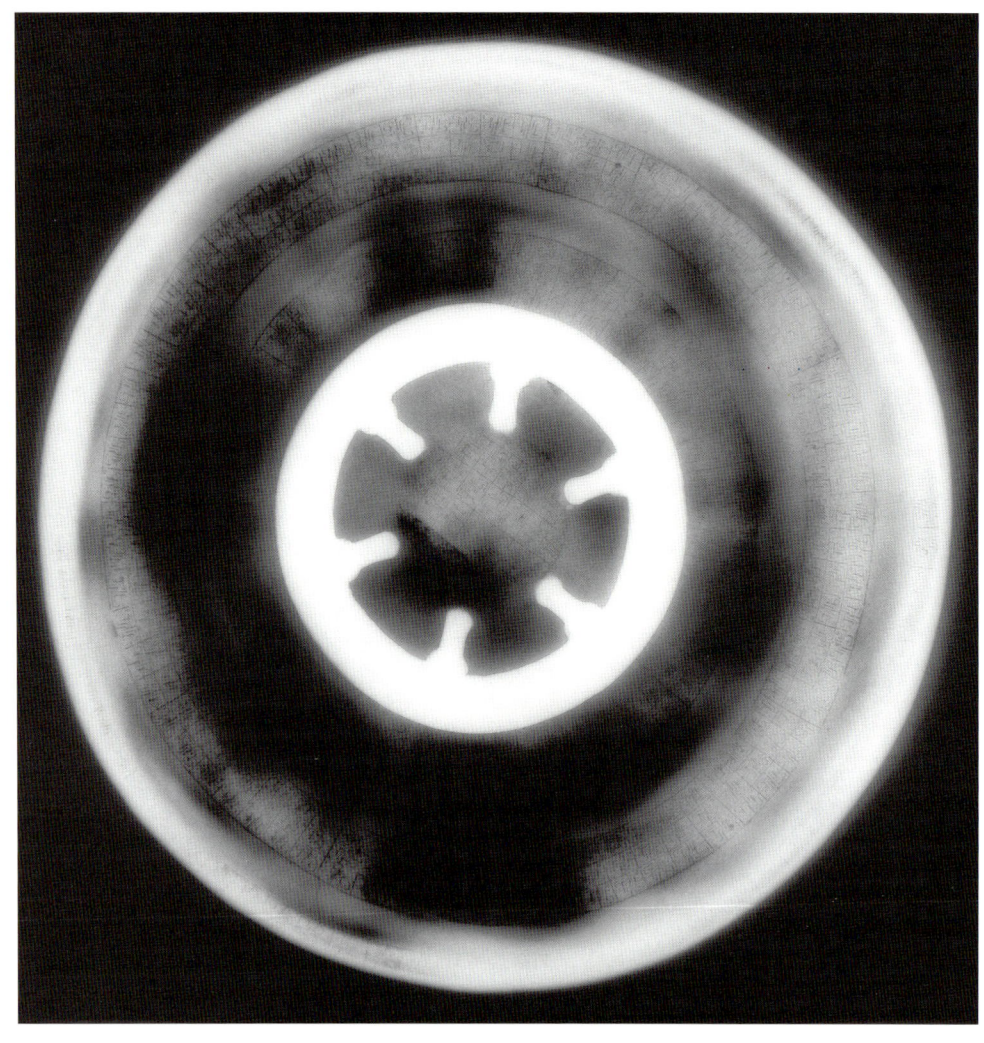

Fig. 218 X-ray of Fake Dou

Description: Yi Wine Jug
Size: 210mm L
Period: Circa 2000 AD

Fig. 219 Fake Yi Wine Jug

The fake yi wine jug (Fig. 219) copies an Eastern Zhou original. The appearance of two casting pin holes shown in the x-ray (Fig. 14) are an immediate give-away, as are the white patches of salts in the corrosion, and the black exposed patches of the bronze body. These pin holes will usually indicate that either lost wax or lost foam casting has been used, and recently at that.

Fig. 220 Underside View of Fake Yi

The close-up of the salts (Fig. 221) also shows the patches where patina did not hold; similar in some respects to bald patches found on some real archaic bronzes.

Fig. 221 Close-up of Salts on Fake

Description: Fake Cover From Yi
Size: 183mm L
Period: Circa 2000AD

Fig. 222 Fake Cover from Yi Wine Ewer

The elaborately decorated lid from a Yi wine ewer (Fig. 222), also copies an original in a Chinese museum collection. The underside view (Fig. 223), and the end on view (Fig. 224) show a feature one would expect to see on the original; namely recesses following the external shape (as the ancient moulds were made of clay). Gettens has noted that these recesses were to minimise shrinkage during the casting operation. Note again on this fake, the pattern has been high-lighted by dirt and corrosion.

Fig. 223 Inside View **Fig. 224 Frontal View**

The x-ray (Fig. 225) again shows an absence of the faults which are detected on the originals.

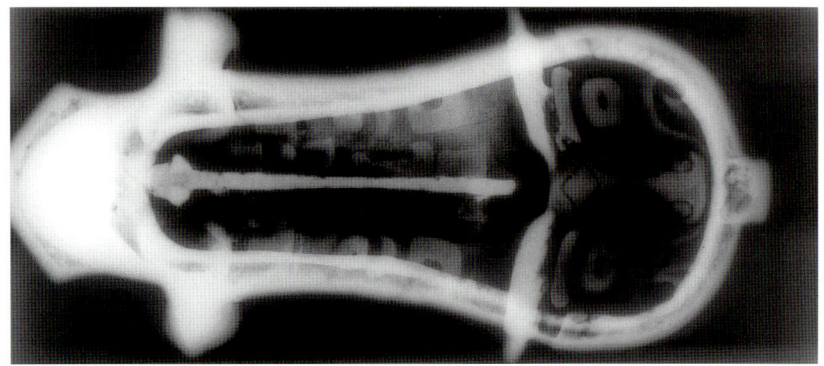

Fig. 225 X-ray of Fake Yi Lid

Many of these better quality bronze copies are being made by the Taiyuan Bronze Culture Research Unit, part of whose brochure I have illustrated (Fig. 226).

Fig. 226 Taiyuan Bronze Culture Research Institute Brochure

Description: Fake Tiger
Size: 205mm L
Period: Circa 2000AD

Fig. 227 Fake Bronze Tiger

Animal figures are arguably among the most expensive bronze subjects on the market, and as a consequence, attract a good deal of the copyist's attention; as the tiger (Fig. 227) illustrates. Note the deliberately broken tail and the relatively crude attempt at patination and decoration (Fig. 228).

Fig. 228 Close-up of Fake Patina

The bronzes illustrated (Fig. 229, 230, 231, and 232), came from a dishonest Hong Kong mail-order company, the activities of which I wrote about in a magazine article in 1996. These were high quality fakes, some with gold and silver inlay that compared with the Warring States originals.

Fig. 229 Fake Bronze Figures

Fig. 230 A Variety of Fake Inlaid Animals & a Belt Hook

Fig. 231 More Fake Bronzes

Fig. 232 Fake Inlaid Dragon

The gilded vessel (Fig. 231) was readily identifiable as a fake, because it had not been cast. Purportedly Tang dynasty (618 to 906AD), it was as patently fake as the jade handled sword, the patina (corrosion) on which has been glued to the blade. The inlaid dragon (Fig. 232) is a work of art in itself, copies an original piece in a Chinese museum publication, and undoubtedly will be the antique of tomorrow.

It is interesting to see the numbers and range of new fakes becoming available, many copying known originals in major museum collections or auction catalogues; others, like the applied studs to a Warring States period amphora (Fig. 233), just a figment of a fraudster's imagination. In this case, the studs probably came from an ancient horse livery or harness, but they certainly enliven these ancient amphorae; sufficiently to fool one major U.S. auction house.

Description: "Swirling Eye" Amphora
Size: 185mm H
Period: Warring States (475 to 221BC)

Fig. 233 Warring States Amphora with Applied Bronze Studs

In a Chinese warehouse I secretly took a photograph (Fig. 234) of a number of these amphorae, the studs newly applied with automotive panel beaters "bog". In this rare case however, both the studs and the amphorae individually were genuine archaic pieces; just combined to be more saleable today. Readers must be alert to composite bronzes; pieces made with either a mixture of genuine, but unrelated parts, or a mixture of genuine and fake parts. Here again, x-ray is an invaluable tool.

Fig. 234 Amphorae with Newly Applied Studs

In general, the patination of the fakes appears to be deteriorating, many modern day copyists preferring to make a cursory attempt at duplicating the original patina. This is good news for the serious collector, as it makes authentication and fake detection much simpler. But some manufacturers go to a lot of trouble, as the wonderful tiger head (Fig. 235) evidences.

Description: Tiger's Head
Size: 195mm H
Period: Circa 2000AD

Fig. 235 Fake Tiger's Head

Hopefully the close-up of the patina on this well executed fake (Fig. 236) will be of assistance to many of my readers, as it appears on numbers of better quality fake bronzes available in the market today. The major feature to note is the overall consistency of the green colour, the tendency to flake, and the patches of yellow among the green.

Fig. 236 Close-up of Fake Patina

It must be remembered that many of the modern copies of ancient bronzes are made using the "lost wax", or more recently, the "lost foam" method of casting. With these methods, much more detailed castings can be made than with the traditional clay moulds, the molten bronze replacing a melted wax or foam model. The "lost wax" method was used by the Chinese from circa the sixth century BC, but only rarely, and then only on the most elaborate vessels or fittings. The appearance of pins or pin holes to stabilize the mould during pouring, is often an indicator of the use of this method.

One final point to mention, which may be of assistance to readers, who unlike the author, have a sense of smell, is to try an old Chinese test for antiquity. Pour a little boiling water into the inside of any allegedly old vessel; say a hu jar or ding, and swirl it around. Provided the vessel has not been over-cleaned, the smell should be that of dank caves.

I have also heard it asserted that those with acute senses of smell can detect glue, used perhaps for attaching ground up scrapings of patina to cover repairs. With regard to glue, I must mention the possibility of dirt being mixed with glue, especially to cover repairs, but sometimes to simulate genuine dirt; which on ancient bronzes often binds almost inextricably with the corrosion, and can be extremely difficult to remove.

For those readers who do not travel regularly in China, I have concluded this chapter with three photographs (Fig. 237 to 239) of a bronze stall in the Guangzhou Jadewares Market. It gives some idea of the range and quantity of fake bronzes being produced.

Fig. 237 Fake Bronzes in the Guangzhou Jadewares Market

Fig. 238 & 239 Fake Bronzes in the Guangzhou Jadewares Market

CHAPTER 15

CONCLUSION

As I read the final draft of this book, I realise the deficiencies within it. I have no doubt that I will be slated by academics for daring to invade their private space, and castigated by metallurgical and other allegedly scientific laboratories for sometimes disputing their assertions. The initial response to my first book on later Chinese porcelain was the same, and I have no doubt that while this book will be similarly dismissed by my many academic critics, hopefully the serious collectors and dealers, to whom it is aimed, will appreciate my comments, observations and often frank suggestions.

The authentication of ancient Chinese bronzes is an inexact science, and will remain so until such time as the wealth of knowledge, gained from the ongoing excavations in China, are properly documented and translated into English.

In the meantime, collectors will need to remain on their guard for the ever-present problem of fakes, and in that regard I have compiled a simple checklist of features to look for and aspects to consider, both positive and negative, which may assist in authentication. These are:

Azurite blue patina inside & underneath.
Bald patches.
Carbonaceous materials in the corrosion (ie wood, lacquer etc).
Clay (fired) cores.
Corrosion (White patches etc).
Defects (eg out of round).
Fabric in the corrosion.
Fire (soot) remains on dings & other cooking vessels.
Food remains inside food vessels.
Frozen joints.
Inlay.
Inscriptions.
Inward bending rims.
Misalignment of decoration.
Mould lines.
Price in relation to rarity.
Rarity.
Repairs.
Restoration.
Rust stains.
Spacers (chaplets).
Sprue marks.
Tree or plant roots.
Vent marks.
Watermarks

Remember my earlier advice to look for what is not there, that one would reasonably expect to see. If there is any doubt, best advice is not to buy it; or buy it with a written guarantee and right of return. Nowadays, if I have any doubts, I will usually discipline myself to leave it unpurchased.

Readers can assess from the illustrations, and my on-line auctions, the numbers of pieces of Chinese bronze that I get to handle in the course of a year; well over 500. And I regularly come across items that I am uncertain of, especially those pieces which have been cleaned of the corrosion, and items I have never previously encountered. Some, like the curious two handled cauldron (Fig. 239), while undoubtedly genuine (probably Western Han), had a domestic use and will seldom be found illustrated. It is because of undocumented pieces like this, that copyists are able to get away with some of their often elaborate inventions, disposing of them to a gullible public.

Description: **Cauldron**
Size: **200mm D**
Period: **Western Han**
(206BC to 9AD)

Fig. 239 Han Dynasty Cauldron

Of the scientific testing procedures currently available to establish the age of a bronze, thermoluminescence testing is in my view the most reliable. But this only works on fired clay cores of bases, lugs and legs, and as I earlier explained, the results can be distorted by outside factors; repair, x-ray and even downright dishonesty.

Carbon 14 dating, because of its cost, is going to be restricted to the most valuable bronzes, and again the results may be unreliable. From my perspective, I am happy to continue buying from sources that have proved historically to be reliable, and readers could well do to follow this advice. I continue to double-check my purchases, looking for corroborative signs of authenticity, and periodically backing my evaluations with thermoluminescence tests and x-rays.

The bronze spear heads (Fig. 240 to 242) serve to emphasise the "corroborative" point, for the central Western Zhou spear head has clear evidence of the original binding, while the lower Warring states period example has the remains of the original wood shaft; two aspects one is unlikely to find with any modern fake. Note also the mixed azurite/malachite patina of the uppermost late Shang/early Western Zhou example, and the distinct red (copper) colour of the middle spear head; the latter colour being a recurring feature of many weapons of the Shang period.

Description: Three Spear Heads
Size: 185 to 220mm
Period: Late Shang to Warring States

Fig.240 Three Early Bronze Spear Heads

Fig. 241 Close-up of Binding

Fig. 242 Close-up of Wood Shaft Remains

As I concluded the final chapter of this book, one of my regular suppliers offered me a group of twelve of these strange arrow heads, five of which are illustrated (Fig. 243). He assured me that they were originally made like this to fire from a crossbow. However, the majority consensus of a group of weapons collectors shown these pieces, suggests that they are a composite piece; a Western Zhou arrow head and an Eastern Zhou or Han parasol tip. On breaking one apart, I found a bamboo splint inside, as can be seen in the lower right example. Why anybody would go to the trouble of fabricating these, is beyond me.

I personally remain to be convinced that these tubular fittings with the hook were in fact parasol tips, as a more plausible explanation is that they were the ends of crossbow arrows, the wood shaft of which has rotted. The reason I suggest this possibility, is that whenever I am offered them they invariably are in quantity with arrow heads (not normally attached). They also come in various sizes, as do the crossbow mechanisms, and seem to fit perfectly into the rounded slot adjacent to the trip mechanism.

Fig. 243 Composite Arrow Heads

The sheer audacity of some of these fake sellers never ceases to amaze me, and at the risk of upsetting one collector whom I have met, I relate a story told to me by him. He has been buying allegedly genuine bronzes in China (Beijing), including from a dealer with the "secret" tomb. However, one day while working on a construction project, his digger unearthed a massive bronze horse. For a fee he was allowed to keep it, and the horse was smuggled out to New Zealand. I suggested that he get it x-rayed, and to his amazement, not mine, it showed modern repairs and lost wax pin holes. This horse, if genuine, would have been worth perhaps $US1 million. Others of his bronzes were also fakes, but included were some which appeared to me to be genuine, but with modern decoration.

One of the latest bronzes acquired by me was the curious jia (Fig. 134), with its strange flat lid and relatively constant patina. I was unable to find a similar example illustrated in any books in my reference library, and instinctively suspicious and concerned that it may not be genuine, or at the very least, restored, I had it x-rayed. The first x-ray (Fig. 244) of the base showed spacers and casting faults, the second (Fig. 245) through the side showed the same, and the third of the lid, yet another spacer (Fig. 246), and the expected irregularities from the ancient pour.

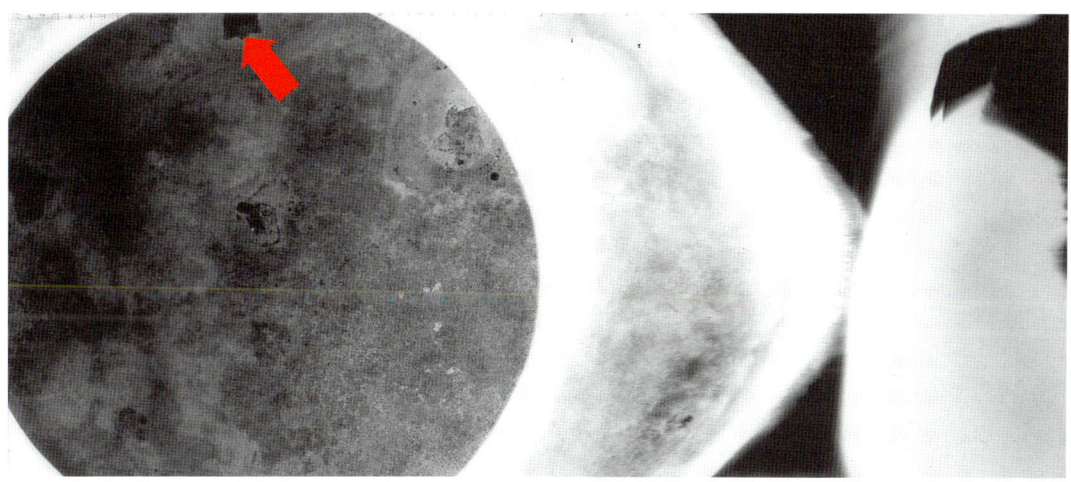

Fig. 244 X-ray of Base of Jia

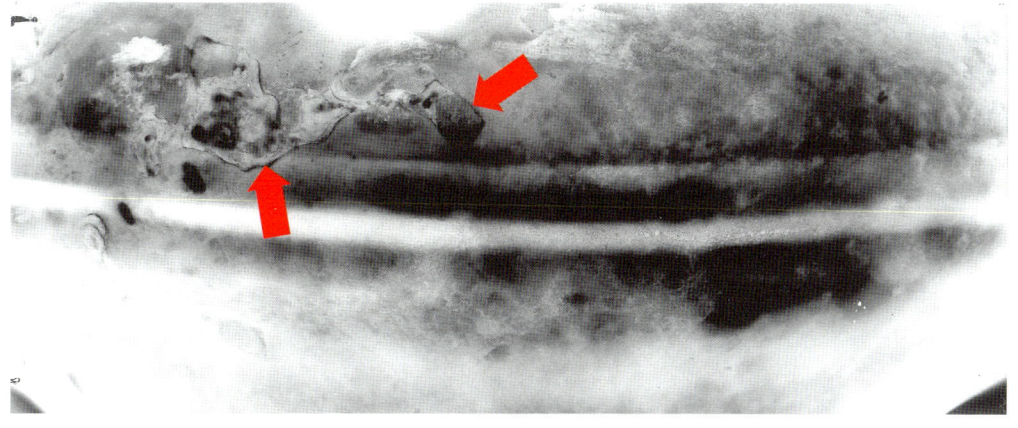

Fig. 245 X-ray of Side of Jia

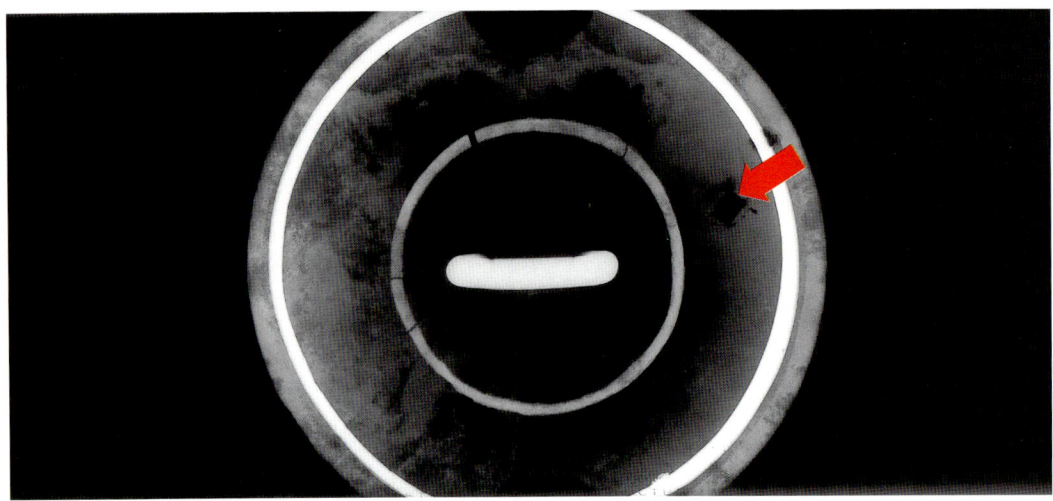

Fig. 246 X-ray of Lid of Jia

The combination of the internal water mark, plus the evidence of ancient casting methods from the x-rays, convinced me on this occasion that the bronze jia was neither restored, nor was it a modern copy; despite the fact that I could not find a similar example. I wish that every piece which I evaluate to buy was as easy as this one, for many are not.

The miniature bronze ding or cauldron (Fig. 247) is another example of a piece I have yet to see illustrated elsewhere. Possibly made as a child's toy, it has taotie mask legs, with a most penetrating gaze (Fig. 248)

Description: Miniature Ding
Size: 65mm H
Period: Probably Warring States (475 to 221BC)

Fig. 247 Miniature Bronze Ding   Fig.248 Close-up of Taotie Mask

If I have not made this point abundantly clear already, let me say again that collectors or dealers in ancient Chinese bronzes should always keep an open mind; open to the possibility that a piece may be genuine, and open to the possibility that it may be fake. The final piece that I have available to illustrate (Fig. 249), a miniature fanghu wine jar, is a case in point. It has the following positive indicators of authenticity:

1. It is a classic Warring States or Han size and shape.
2. It has a good azurite blue and malachite green patina.
3. There is fabric embedded in the corrosion.(Fig.250)
4. There is hardened slime on the inside.(Fig. 251)

Description: Miniature Fanghu Wine Jar
Size: 175mm H
Period: Warring States or Western Han
(475BC to 9AD)

Fig. 249 Warring States or Han Dynasty Fanghu Wine Jar

Fig. 250 Fabric in Corrosion   **Fig.251 Hardened Slime on Inside**

But it has a gold inscription on one side (Fig.252). However, the area immediately around the inscription is a bright malachite green, totally at variance with the other malachite areas of corrosion. The other point to note is that the gold has been filed flat to level with the bronze.

Conclusion: the hu is an ancient piece, but the inscription has been added in recent times.

Fig. 252 Inscription

This brings me back to the **"considered opinion"** which I have referred to earlier in this book. The majority of the bronzes which I buy come from two reputable sources, and 99% of them have satisfied these dealers as to their authenticity. In assessing bronzes for purchase, whether from these two dealers or otherwise, I still look for the pointers of confirmation which I have enumerated earlier. Some other features, like the weight, come only from experience.

My final advice to collectors and dealers who take the plunge into the fascinating world of ancient Chinese bronzes, is *"If you are not 100% certain that the piece in question is genuine, then leave it and buy something else. At least for the present, there is a lot to choose from."*

I trust that nothing I have said in this book will discourage anyone from taking advantage of the fabulous opportunities which exist at present to assemble a major collection of ancient Chinese bronzes. I do not for a moment think that this extraordinary situation will continue indefinitely.

The compilation of this book has no been an easy task. I do not have a museum full of exhibits to illustrate, but an ever changing range of stock, necessitating numerous trips to the photographer before the items are sold on the internet auctions. I see in this final draft that I have carelessly duplicated two illustrations, but if I am to get this book printed before Christmas 2001, I do not have time to rectify this mistake. Nor do I have time, as much as I would have liked, to include illustrations of my latest purchases, including 25 rare bronze dagger-axes (ge) from a hoard found in Sichuan province.

Having finished this book, I now await the opinions and comments of readers. There will undoubtedly be corrections to be made in any subsequent reprinting. I welcome constructive comments and criticism, and may be contacted:

A.J. (Tony) Allen,
Allen's Enterprises Ltd,
P.O. Box 33-194,
Takapuna,
Auckland,
New Zealand

Ph/Fax: +64-9-479-3960
Email: Allen.Ent@xtra.co.nz
Web-site: www.allensantiques.com

SELECTED BIBLIOGRAPHY

1. **Chinese Bronzes Generally:**

   English Text:

   Ackerman, Phyllis;
   "Ritual Bronzes Of Ancient China", 1945.

   Art Institute of Chicago,
   "Chinese Bronzes From The Buckingham Collection", 1946

   Barnard, Noel;
   Bronze Casting & Bronze Alloys In Ancient China, 1961.

   Bussagli, Mario;
   "Chinese Bronzes", 1966.

   Kuwayama, George (Los Angeles County Museum Of Art);
   "The Great Bronze Age Of China – A Symposium", 1983.

   Lefebvre D' Argence, Rene-Yvon;
   "Bronze Vessels Of Ancient China In The Avery Brundage Collection", 1977.

   Li Xueqin,
   "Chinese Bronzes. A General Introduction", 1995.

   ***Pope, Gettens, Cahill & Barnard;**
   "The Freer Chinese Bronzes, Vol. 1 & 2", 1968.

   Rawson, Jessica
   "Western Zhou Ritual Bronzes From The Arthur M. Sackler Collections", 1990

   Rawson, Jessica & **Bunker,** Emma;
   "Ancient Chinese & Ordos Bronzes", 1990.

   Wain, Peter;
   "Miller's Chinese & Japanese Antiques Buyer's Guide, 1999.

   Watson, William,
   "Ancient Chinese Bronzes", 1962.

   ***Wen Fong;**
   "The Great Bronze Age Of China, 1980.

   William Rockhill Nelson Gallery Of Art, et al.
   "The Chinese Exhibition. The Exhibition Of Archaeological Finds Of The People's Republic Of China", 1975.

English & Chinese Text:
> **Hong Kong Museum Of Art & Hebei Provincial Museum;**
> "Warring States Treasures. Cultural Relics From The State Of Zhongshan, Hebei Province", 1999.
> **Li Xueqin**
> 'The Glorious Traditions Of Chinese Bronzes", 2000.
> **The Alumni Association Of The University Of Nanking;**
> "Illustrated Catalogue Of Chinese Government Exhibits For The International Exhibition Of Chinese Art In London", 1936.

Chinese Text:
> **Ji Chongjian,**
> "Ancient Bronzes", 1999.
> ***Li Jiangwei & Nu Ruihong,**
> "Photographic List Of Chinese Bronzes", 2000.
> ***Peng Qingyun et al, (National Antique Bureau)**
> "Dictionary Of China's Most Famous Antiques, Bronze Volume", 1995.

2. **Chinese Bronze Weapons:**
English & Chinese Text:
> ***National Palace Museum;**
> "Illustrated Catalogue Of Ancient Bronze Weaponry In The National Palace Museum", 1995.
> ***Wang, C.H.;**
> "Shang & Zhou Chinese Bronze Weaponry", 1993.

Chinese Text:
> ***Cheng Dong & Zhong Shao-yi;**
> "Ancient Chinese Weapons – A Collection Of Pictures", 1990.

3. **Chinese Bronze Coins:**
English Text:
> **Jen,** David;
> "Chinese Cash. Identification & Price Guide", 2000.

Chinese Text:
Ding Fubao, (Shanghai Book Shop),
"Ancient Chinese Coins", 1986.
Liu Juchen,
"Illustrative Plates Of Chinese Ancient Coins", 1989.

4. **Chinese Bronze Mirrors:**
   Chinese Text:
   Da Kang,
   "Decorated Historic Bronze Mirrors (By North River Publishing Co)", 1996.

*Recommended.

INDEX

acetone; 51,
air bubbles; 19, 39, 61, 92,
afterlife; 12,
ancestor worship; 12,
animal heads; 128,
Anyang phase; 12,
arrow heads; 129, 160,
arsenic; 37,
authentication techniques; 19, 57, 157,
axe heads; 130, 135,
azurite; 54, 81, 119, 130,
bald patches; 68, 131,
Barnard, N; 18,
bells; 125,
belt (or garment) hooks; 125, 126,
binding (remains); 63, 64, 140, 142, 143, 159,
bo shan lu; 117,
botryoidal malachite; 53,
bridle bits; (see horse bridle bits)
bronze casting; 15,
bronze formula; 15,
bronze history; 11,
burial conditions; 55,
Bushell, Stephen; 15,
buttons; 126,
cadmium; 37,
Cantonese; 7,
carbon; 16,
carbon 14 dating; 20, 47-48,
carbonaceous debris; 64,
casting marks; 41,
cauldron; 158, 162,
censer; 116-118,
cerussite; 51, 54,
chains; 85,
chaplets; (see spacers),
charcoal; 47,
chariot axle hubs; 66, 115, 126,
chemical analysis; 19,
Chinese historical texts; 8, 15,

Chinese language; 7,
cire perdue; 18, (see also lost wax)
clay cores; 19, 42, 60, 70, 92, 101,
clay moulds; 15,
coins; 120,
composites; 56,
concubines; 12, 115,
copper content; 15,
copper inlay; 61,
copper smelting; 12,
corrosion; 20, 41, 51-56,
corruption; 44-46,
crossbow mechanisms; 66, 136,
cuprite; 52, 146, 147,
dagger; 136, 137,
dagger axe; (see ge),
damage; 66, 67, 80,
dating from shape & design; 21,
decoration, quality of; 61,
design; 19, 21,
ding; 13, 22, 73-86, 162,
dirt; 65,
dishonesty; 9,
dou; 22, 86, 146,
dovetailing; 17,
drainage loop; 105,
dragon head handles; 92,
dui; 23, 84,
Eastern Han; 11,
Eastern Zhou; 11,
emerald green; 52,
Emperor; 12,
Erligang culture; 12,
Erlitou culture; 11,
error ratio; 10,
fabric in the corrosion; 20, 47, 50, 65, 121, 163,
fake(s); 10, 13, 50, 121, 137, 145-156,
fanghu; 87, 163,
fang lei; 23,
fang yi; 24,

fat remains; 47,
fire; 16,
fish, twin design; 109-110,
flaws; 19, 74, 75, 93, 139,
food remains; 47,
Freer Chinese Bronzes; 9,
frozen joints; 66,
fu; 24,
garlic head hu; 27, 104,-107,
garment hooks; 125,
garniture, tomb; 115,
ge; 129-133,
glued patina; 51,
gold inlay; 72, 164,
gong (guang); 25,
gu; 25, 88-90,
Guangzhou Jadewares Market; 155-156,
gui; 26, 91, 94, 95,
Han dynasty; 11,
he; 26, 96,
hill censer; 117,
holes (for mould brackets); 68, 90,
horse bridle bits; 67, 125,
hu; 27, 67, 96-107,
impurities; 39,
inlay; 17, 61, 70-72, 96, 97, 137, 138,
inscriptions; 69, 70, 164,
jade; 63,
jia; 27, 107, 161, 162,
jian; 28,
jiao; 28,
jue; 29,
kaishu; 7,
K'ao Kung Chi; 15,
king; 12, 13,
lacquer; 47, 63, 71,
ladles; 127,
laminated edges; 55,
lamps; 118-119,
lead-based solder; 49,
lead content; 12, 36,
lead smear; 36,

lead substitutes; 13,
lei; 29,
leiwen; 21, 57, 90,
li; 30, 108,
Li Xueqin; 8,
lost foam; (see lost wax),
lost wax; 18, 42, 155,
lugs; 95,
malachite; 51, 53, 81,
mandarin; 7,
manganese; 37,
metallurgical analysis; 19, 35–38,
microscopy; 20, 35, 49, 50,
mirrors; 121-125,
mould lines; 16, 41, 57, 110,
National Palace Museum, Taipei; 55,
nickel; 37,
painted patina; 138,
pan; 30, 109,
panel-beaters' "bog"; 66, 153,
parasol tips; 160,
Paris green; 52,
patination & re-patination; 20, 40, 50, 51-56, 155,
pinyin; 7,
PIXE; 38,
pole arm feet; 143,
polished bronze; 56, 82,
pommel (on sword); 50, 138,
Pope, Gettens, Cahill & Barnard; 9,
pottery cores (see clay cores);
pottery replicas; 12, 115,
pou; 31,
price; 145,
Price, David; 46-47,
Prussian blue; 52,
putonghua; 7,
Qin dynasty; 11,
radiography; 39-42,
repairs; 19, 20, 40, 49, 50, 52, 65, 102,
rims (inward bending); 16, 68, 100,
ring handled swords; 142,
rituals; 13,

Romanisation; 7,
rust stains; 68, 113,
sacrifices; 12,
salts; 149,
scabbard remains; 138, 141,
scanning, digital; 20,
Shang dynasty; 11,
shapes; 21,
silicon; 37,
silver inlay; 72,
slime (hardened); 68, 163,
smalt; 52,
smell; 155,
smithying; 15,
solvents; 51, 88,
soot; 47, 58, 73,
spacers; 15, 16, 17, 39, 58, 61, 83, 102, 162,
spear head; 46, 65, 133-135, 159,
Spence, Jonathon D; 8,
Spring & Autumn; 11,
sprue marks; 16, 17, 41, 59, 77,
stoves; 120,
"swirling eye" amphora; 153,
swords; 137-142,
sword guards; 144,
sword handles; 62, 138, 143,
Taiyuan Bronze Culture Research Unit; 151,
taotie (lion mask); 21, 100, 102, 103, 162,
textiles (see fabric),
thermoluminescence testing; 20, 43-47, 158,
tiger; 151, 154,
tin content; 37, 55,
tin oxide corrosion; 55,
tombs; 13, 55,
tool signature; 49,
transliteration; 7,
tree or plant roots; 20, 65,

trellis lines; 68,
troves; 13,
turquoise inlay; 72, 137,
ultra-violet light; 51,
ultramarine (artificial); 52,
undercut designs; 17,
value of bronze; 13,
value (sale); 19,
vent marks; 16, 17, 59, 60,
Wade-Giles; 7, 8,
Wang Mang Interregnum; 11,
Warring States; 11,
water or wine stains; 68,
weapons; 129-144,
wear; 67,
welding; 17,
Western Han; 11,
Western Zhou; 11,
wet preservation; 101,
wet testing; 36,
Wollongong University; 46,
wood (in the corrosion); 20, 47, 64, 78, 204, 160,
wood shafts (remains); 63,
x-ray analysis; 17, 19, 39-42, 52, 66, 89, 92, 109, 110, 121, 139, 148, 161,
x-ray diffraction; 38,
Xia dynasty; 11, 12,
xian; 31, 111-113,
yan; 31, 111-113,
yellow; 155,
yi; 32, 114, 148,
Yinxu culture; 12,
you; 32,
yu; 33,
zhan; 33,
zhi; 34,
Zhou dynasty; 11,
zinc; 37,
zun; 34,

NOTES

NOTES

NOTES

NOTES